Anne Beale

Country Landlords

Volume 2

Anne Beale

Country Landlords
Volume 2

ISBN/EAN: 9783337314033

Printed in Europe, USA, Canada, Australia, Japan

Cover: Foto ©Suzi / pixelio.de

More available books at **www.hansebooks.com**

COUNTRY LANDLORDS.

BY

L. M. S.

AUTHOR OF

"GLADYS OF HARLECH."

IN THREE VOLUMES.

VOL. II.

LONDON:
T. C. NEWBY, PUBLISHER,
30, WELBECK STREET CAVENDISH SQUARE.

1860.

With the concluding words, Mrs. Parry hurried away as suddenly as she had appeared at the door.

Gertrude bowed assent without taking her eyes off the chalk portrait on which she was bestowing great pains in working in a shadow that produced a magical effect about the eyes. It so fixed her attention, that she did not lay down her crayons till the whole party were in the room, and Lord Morlif's courteous voice, accompanied with his usual levity of manner, broke upon her ear.

"Ah! here the fairy is, alone in her castle. What a charming effect! quite scenical—quite so, with that lovely marine landscape in the perspective."

Gertrude rose, and did the honours of the lady of the house, with her quiet, unpretending manner.

"A sweet face—what speaking eyes! Is this a copy?" inquired Lord Morlif, looking first attentively at the portrait, and then glancing across the table, as if searching for the original.

" No."

" From life? I was not aware you were such an artist."

" Oh no! not from life."

" What! from imagination? Surely you are joking."

Gertrude smiled. Was there anything new in drawing from imagination? To her the charm consisted in painting the pictures impressed upon her own mind, which no one else could see. There was a fascination, too, in working up the expressions in the faces she created.

While they were discussing this question, Miss Morlif drew her father's attention to a portrait of Captain Lewis in his naval dress, and remarked what a noble, handsome face it was. She then turned to Gertrude and asked who it was.

" My father."

" Your father!—how unlike you are to

him. Singular he should be so dark, and you so blond."

Gertrude said she was like her mother, who was extremely fair.

" Who was your mother?" interjected Miss Morlif, in an affected and absent manner.

Gertrude coloured. It was an unpleasant question. Lord Morlif was standing near, watching her minutely. The second Miss Morlif had stepped up to the piano, and was turning over some music, and humming the tune of a new song she had heard of, but had not seen before.

" Will you let me try your instrument, Miss Lewis?" said she, happily interrupting their conversation. " It would be a treat, for at present we have not a piano at Bryn-y-Coed."

On gaining permission, she took off her gloves and seated herself.

" If you are going to strum, Miss Lewis will perhaps step out with us upon the terrace—the far-famed terrace," said Lord Morlif. " Of all things, a new song in Mary's hands. It would try the patience of Job !"

·The last sentence was said in an undertone, and as he walked along the terrace he continued—

" Do you know, Miss Lewis, it is a great misfortune in a young lady's education when she has not been taught to know whether she has, or has not, a voice. We poor men are sad martyrs sometimes. I would rather put clay in my ears than sit out one of Mary's screeching songs. Yet there is no making her comprehend that she has no voice. Rose has a slight touch of the nightingale, and has the good sense to know when she has given us enough. I should not have vouchsafed so free an opinion upon the subject, had I not known that Miss Lewis possesses a voice that a *Prima-donna* might envy ; and yet she so rarely indulges us."

As they stood upon the terrace, the aroma

of the blossoming shrubs perfumed the air; and the bees, which seemed to have congregated from all parts of the country, were paying especial court to a large myrtle-tree, speckled with bloom, which reached halfway up to the gable end of the house.

"How beautifully luxuriant everything grows here! It seems to me you have stolen a leaf out of Italy: the *tout ensemble* reminds me of those lovely villas on Lake Como," said Lord Morlif, seating himself by Gertrude, who had escaped out of the rays of a hot July sun to a rustic chair in the shade.

"Papa is extremely attached to Italy: he likes to have things around him to remind him of that unhappy country. This sheltered spot I call papa's corner. Everything thrives here." A suppressed sigh accompanied the last sentence.

"Was that sigh for Italy, or for your father? More for your father than for Italy, I suspect. Do you want him home?"

" Every day, and every hour !" exclaimed Gertrude with emphasis.

" He indulges you to a great extent, I am told," remarked Lord Morlif, in an abstracted manner. After a pause, he continued—

" Your father, I understand, is clever, fascinating, and dangerous."

" Dangerous !" repeated Gertrude.

" Did I say dangerous? Well, it does not require cavilling about ; the word suits admirably. His fine beard and handsome face take the ladies by storm. There is no resisting him ;—so he is dangerous."

" I don't think, my lord, that was quite what you meant. My father seldom goes into society. The word is inapposite."

" Inapposite—*mal-àpropos*, you think. I must be on my guard, I see, with those sweet lips so ready to shield her father. You cannot tell what he was some years ago. You are the centre of attraction now, and it makes a material difference. With a face such as yours to look at every day, any man ought to be contented."

Gertrude felt annoyed and uncomfortable; she wished he would keep his basilisk eyes from off her face, and leave his silly compliments unsaid. "Excuse me; I must go for my hat, that I may join Miss Morlif: she is walking alone."

"Oh, pray don't go; we don't want any hats—that barbarous custom! It is all very well for an ugly face, but an insult to a pretty one. I could swear when I know a lovely face to be under the broad brim and I cannot get a peep at it. Let me beg of you to sit down again. I want you to tell me what this flower is; and I have other questions to ask. Why are you always in such a hurry to get away from me? Now do not tantalize me any more by fluttering about like a butterfly, or drooping like a snowdrop: but let me see you as I did a moment ago, with that dignified look, when we were speaking about your father; that irresistible little mouth drawn up, I don't say distorted. If you could only get those pouting lips into your portrait, I would present the fair artist with a hundred guineas."

" Let me go," said Gertrude, with a deep colour in her face, and endeavouring to draw her girdle from him, which he in a playful manner had taken hold of, and was thus keeping her a prisoner. "I dislike this absurd conversation; and liberties, my lord, are what I never allow."

"Ten thousand pardons; I intended no offence. I am afraid, Miss Lewis, I am given to talking nonsense. But, consider what a pleasant break it is in a man's daily routine, to have a little *badinage* with fair ladies. Heaven knows what dry stuff we men discuss over our bottles, hammering upon a given subject till it is threadbare, and debating about this or that political movement, which would be better left to sleep out its existence untouched by us, for the little good we do it. If we indulge in trifles when we come among the opposite sex, it is unjust to condem us. Some allowances ought surely to be made for us. You must try and get rid of these prudish, primitive ideas. Had those sage words dropped from the lips of some stately dowager or matter-of-fact old maid, it would have been in keeping; but from yours, my young friend, with those laughing eyes, it is positively ridiculous. Nay, now, don't frown upon me. Some day you will better understand these affairs, and enjoy life the more. What did you remark about that flower?"

Gathering two or three different kinds of the same plant, Gertrude was about to explain what she meant, when her companion, not noticing the flowers in her hand, interrupted her.

"As you stood there, gathering those flowers, I could imagine you to be Proserpine, and the god Pluto showed his taste in stealing her out of the garden and making her his queen. Miss Lewis, it is lamentable you should be 'wasting your sweetness in the desert air'—a desert in point of society. You should come to London, and you will soon learn to value what nature has endowed you with. What! frowning your disapproval again! Does not beauty exact a tribute? Pray take the compliments as they are intended. You must, indeed, come to London and enjoy life."

Gertrude answered decidedly, that she had no desire to go into the fashionable world, that a town life to her would be more dull than the country. There was a charm in freedom.

"'Better an outlaw than not free.' Is that it? Well, I own you live in an enviable spot, and have greater freedom and greater indulgences than other young ladies. Still, you don't know the pleasures of life, not the real pleasures."

"Tastes vary. My enjoyments may be greater than you estimate them; higher, perhaps, in point of value, than what you denominate the real pleasures of life."

At that moment, Miss Morlif joined them, and all three returned to the drawing-room. During their absence, Miss Mary Morlif had taken every book out of the music stand, and had made the room look extremely untidy. While the young lady was apologizing, Mrs. Parry suddenly made her appearance and was introduced.

After conversing for some little time, Lord Morlif remarked, in a casual manner, that Captain Lewis had a fine collection of pictures.

" His prime pictures are in the library," said Mrs. Parry. " Have our visitors seen them, Gertrude ?"

" No."

" Oh, then they must have that treat. Gentlemen have come from London purposely to see them." Ringing the bell, she gave orders for the blinds to be drawn up, and in a few minutes the whole par y followed Mrs. Parry into the library.

" What an idol of a room!" ejaculated Miss Morlif. " Are you allowed, Miss Lewis, to frequent this *sanctum sanctorum ?*"

" Yes, I prefer it to any in the house."

" I don't marvel. Who would have expected to have come across such a room as this among the mountains of Wales? And your father is so unselfish, that he allows you to take possession of it?"

" Oh dear, yes; Gertrude is a privileged person," interjected Mrs. Parry, raising her eyebrows. " This is quite as much her *sanctum* as her father's. Here the studies go on, while I am never allowed to put my head beyond the door."

Gertrude stood looking out of the window while her visitors viewed the paintings; she felt annoyed with Mrs. Parry for having brought them there. The room, to her, was a real *sanctum;* her father and Anarawd, the two beings who rested nearest her heart, were associated with everything belonging to it, and she did not wish it to have any other association. She grew impatient for her visitors to depart, she was weary of them.

"Captain Lewis is a good judge of a picture," was the only remark Gertrude heard Lord Morlif make, after he had been standing for a few minutes before the famed landscape.

"This is another which the Captain is particularly partial to," said Mrs. Parry, drawing back the window-curtain, so as to throw a light upon a lovely female portrait, mounted in a handsome gold frame. Lord Morlif looked up. In an instant a slight confusion in the room took place—an unintelligible exclamation had fallen from his lips, and his face was deadly pale. Gertrude looked round, and was startled; and his daughters inquired if he were ill; while Mrs. Parry, for the first time, became silent, then hurried out of the room for water.

" I am sorry you should have given yourself this trouble, my dear madam," said Lord Morlif, as he took the glass of water from her hand. " These sudden seizures do sometimes attack me. The Faculty tell me my heart is affected—don't they, Rose?

He turned to look at some ornaments upon the table, endeavouring to draw their attention from himself.

" A fine figure of bronze you have there, and this ebony cabinet most elaborate—a perfect gem! A bit of Italy again, Miss Lewis! There is no difficulty to discover from whence you come, and from whence so much elegance of taste. The South, the South, we have all borrowed from the voluptuous South – the once-renowned Italy, the cradle of art."

All this was said in a careless tone; but Gertrude, with her discernment, knew he was really much disturbed, and wondered what he could have to do with that portrait.

Two or three times he reminded his

daughters that it was time to go; but they did not appear inclined to quit a spot containing so many attractions. Mrs. Parry's voice once more fell ceaselessly upon the ear, and Miss Morlif importuned Gertrude with numberless questions in connection with herself and the neighbourhood. At length Lord Morlif spoke imperatively to his daughters, and they left the house.

When the door was closed, and Gertrude found herself the sole tenant of the library, her first impulse was to walk deliberately across the room, and station herself before the portrait which had excited Lord Morlif in so unaccountable a manner. She had often been attracted by the face, and in secret wondered why her father would never tell her whom it represented. She was sure it was some one nearly allied to him, but neither his nor her mother's; that he had told her positively: who, then, could it be? It was a beautiful face, beaming with affection and sentiment, and having a good deal of fire about the eyes. The arched and finely-pencilled eyebrow, with that melancholy, very melancholy expression, seemed to tell her that it was one of Italy's fair daughters.

Again and again she glanced at the face; and the more she dwelt upon it, the more was she puzzled how Lord Morlif could be connected with a relative of her father.

"A mystery, and very singular," said she to herself, "that I never look upon this beautiful face, without that room appearing before my vision, with its fresco paintings upon the walls, its tessellated floors, its balcony and rich drapery, and that one giant vine, hanging in festoons from tree to tree, standing in a garden?"

Her meditations at that moment were disturbed by the entrance of Yarico, who approached with a note upon a salver. The negress immediately glanced suspiciously at her mistress, then at the portrait before which they were standing. A strange expression came over her features, which Gertrude instantly noticed, and seized with curiosity she asked her " if she did not think it a beautiful face, and had she ever seen the person that the picture was intended to represent ?"

Yarico's eyes began to move restlessly about their sockets, and vainly endeavoured to conceal the embarrassment which her mistress's words caused her.

" You know, then, Yarico, who it is ; and my father's secret is in your possession, and yet not mine."

" Missus dear will know some day," said the negress, crouching at her feet, and looking up in her face with extreme concern.

This was a quiet acknowledgment that something of moment was kept from her. Not wishing Yarico to know how deeply she felt this disclosure, she took the note, which required an immediate answer, and opened it. It was from Lady Elizabeth, requesting her to go to Bleddyn that evening. She wrote a hurried reply, and placed it in Yarico's hand, and was again left to her own reflections. She did not feel comfortable nor happy: Lord Morlif always spoke of her father with such strange insinuations, throwing as much mystery around her as her father had done with the picture. Why should her father keep anything from her? There was something in Lord Morlif's deep-set eyes which left an uncomfortable impression and augured ill: she wished her father had never left home, that she might then have opened her whole heart to him. Suspicion was an unpleasant companion, a many-headed monster; the quicker he was dismissed the better. The world might deceive her, but not Anarawd, nor her father, fond as he was of mystery.

CHAPTER II.

It was a bright afternoon in the beautiful month of August: Lord Morlif was walking leisurely along the path between Clogwyn and Bleddyn, when he suddenly encountered Mr Gwynne. "What on earth have you been after, running over the fields like a madman?" was his exclamation, as he stood surveying his friend from head to foot, with a ludicrous expression of face; "and what puts you in this delectable state? Have you had a fall?"

"I have. The rascal has escaped me, too, confound him! And confound the gates, I have nearly broken my leg in getting over that rickety thing; one of the poles gave way. That booby M'Farlane, with all his troop of men under him, does not attend to these affairs as he ought to do. I will give him such a dressing some of these days! such as he never had in his life."

"Well, my friend, you seem a little warm. Pray who is this rascal you have been in pursuit of and are anathematising?"

"Warm! enough to make me warm. Have I not been chasing that vagabond poacher for the last half-hour? I only wish I had had my gun with me; as sure as fate I should have peppered his legs for him, and given him something to remember. The impudence of the fellow! positively laying down a gin before my eyes! But I know the man's face: it is that notorious Robin, who has already given me no end of trouble; and I will have him up yet before the magistrates."

"What! in this harmless country are you annoyed by poachers?"

Mr. Gwynne related how he had in several instances suffered by the poachers since he came to live at Bleddyn, and how little chance there was of getting rid of them as long as there were lenient, soft-headed magistrates in the county. He then inquired what had brought his lordship across the fields. Had he been at Clogwyn? it looked suspicious.

" Yes," replied Lord Morlif, placing his hand upon his friend's shoulder. " And, will you believe it? the little witch would not admit me this morning! She has not looked as kindly upon me as I could wish, for some time."

There was no expression to indicate surprise in Mr. Gwynne's face; he only looked annoyed, and bit his lips in silence. Lord Morlif continued—

" Gwynne,"—he paused, then added hurriedly—" we have always been great chums from our college-days; will you give me a helping hand in this affair? When she is at your house, do not forget to invite me ; and—" he hesitated,—" and, throw a little dust in your lady's eyes. You know what I mean ?"

Not even Mr. Gwynne could encounter the sharp underlook which darted from Lord Morlif's deep-set eye, without feeling uncomfortable. He gave him no direct answer, but stood striking his boot with his cane.

Shortly afterwards they crossed the fields together, and entered the drive, Lord Morlif engrossing the whole time with his own affairs. He spoke of Captain Lewis's mal-treatment of him in France, and avowed that he would not rest till he had given him the glorious reprisal he had in store for him.

" I would advise you to consider well what you are about, before you again throw down the gauntlet to Lewis," interrupted Mr. Gwynne. " You should not forget that he had ample provocation for treating you as he did; many, under the circumstances, would have done the same."

Lord Morlif turned sharply round. " Provocation, indeed! What right had that man or any man to interfere with me and my affairs? I had enough from him, I should think! You, of all men in the universe, to defend that self-righteous moralist! It seems, my friend, *you* have forgotten what passed under your roof. Time is fleet of foot; but it does not carry away what it brings, nor does it sweep all traces from recollection, much as we may desire it."

" I defend him! God forbid!" ejaculated Mr. Gwynne, slightly irritated. " But don't let us quarrel about that fellow. You are master of your own actions. I have nothing more to say."

" And answerable for your own actions— you should have finished your sentence. That was what was drummed into my ears from a boy. It never took root; it could not find a genial soil, nor is it likely to do so now. I know how to enjoy life without the aid of doctrine. What fallacy—what humbug there is in the world! But we will change the subject. Where is your son now—not coming home, I hope?"

"Oh, no: he is still leading a vagabond life among the Alps, at some of those wild places. I mean to keep mother and son apart as long as I can."

"What will your lady say to that? how will you pacify her?"

Mr. Gwynne gave an equivocal answer, and laughed.

Lord Morlif continued—

"When are we to have the pleasure of your society at Bryn-y-Coed? You have been a stranger lately."

"I did think of coming to you this evening."

"Then pray don't change your mind—come. I met a fisherman taking up a splendid salmon, just fresh out of the water. We find it difficult to cater in this country. Is it that we are not up to all the local tricks?"

Mr. Gwynne remarked that they brought their goods from town, but his lordship had better send his cook to Bleddyn, and the one would soon put the other in the right way if there was anything to be had in the country."

" Is not that Miss Lewis's horse?" inquired Lord Morlif, a little flurried in manner, on arriving before Bleddyn, and a groom appeared, leading a horse up and down between the stable and the front. On receiving an answer in the affirmative, he immediately hurried to the drawing-room, and found Gertrude sitting with Lady Elizabeth and a friend of her ladyship's, who was on a visit at Bleddyn.

" I am fortunate! You are precisely the person, Miss Lewis, I was wishing to see, that I might inquire about an old woman who has been repeatedly asking for alms. She seems to be in a deplorable state, yet tells me she is your pensioner. That does not look as if the story were true."

He spoke in a careless tone, while he played with Gertrude's whip, which he had picked up from the carpet. On Lady Elizabeth asking what the woman's name was, he laughed, saying—

"Oh, Betty—Betty Jones, or Betty Williams, or Lloyd, one of the three. I shall describe her to Miss Lewis; she will know better by description than by name; for if there is one Betty Williams or Jones, there are twenty or more to be found in the village."

Gertrude had to listen to his description, the whole a fabricated tale merely to suit his purpose.

Lord Morlif's repeated visits at Clogwyn caused a great deal of gossip in the neighbourhood, and many unsparing remarks were aimed at the defenceless Gertrude. Envy upon such occasions is generally at the root, and charity too rarely creeps in to shelter the victim. Yet, if Gertrude had enemies in one class, she had friends in another. This was discoverable in the good old kitchen in the little town of Angharad.

It is a long time since we stepped under the roof where the old sign of the "Llewelyn ap Griffydd" still swings over the door, and the eye rested upon the old oak settle and antique clock. Many events had taken place since then, many visible changes. Babies had grown into children, and children into men, and the old and the infirm had dropped into the grave. The kitchen looked now not quite as it did in those days. One of the clocks was removed—gone, it was said, to grace the walls of the eldest daughter's new home; and the old store of shells, and mugs, kettles, cheese-presses, and toasting-forks, had considerably diminished in number. The blue cotton umbrella, still in existence, now looked very faded indeed. Still there was an air of comfort about the apartment, for that belonged to it, and always would belong to it, while the active, little, sensible hostess presided over it. Hugh, as well as his wife, had lost in some degree their good looks. Time had not run on without interlining his path with cares; but no matter, so long as it did not change the hearts within—and it had not done that. Hugh was the same goodhearted, it may almost be said tender-hearted, man as of old, ready to do a kind act for a friend or neighbour, and as careful and considerate for the beasts in the stall, as he was for the guests round his hearth. All men are selfish, is a phrase constantly heard. Some are ready to dispute the axiom, as in Hugh Lloyd's case, for there never was a less selfish being in the world.

He was at this moment sitting and musing near his window in the kitchen. It was just before the time when the customers drop in to take their evening's pipe and mug of beer. His wife hastened to remove the tea-things off a three-legged table; and having swept away the crumbs with her apron, she took up her knitting, and sat down near her goodman, ready to mingle a little chat with her work.

"Something has come over you, Hugh bach. You not look the same these last few days. Indeed, I hope nothing has gone wrong?" she said, looking at her husband inquiringly.

"Wrong, Molly? Why, yes, to be sure, there is something always going wrong in this world, with a neighbour or among ourselves; always some trouble walking about—only this little difference, that sometimes she come very slow and quiet, and sometimes with a big noise; and, indeed, truth it is very hard to tell which is the ugliest."

"Well, dear anwyl! which is it now, Hugh bach? I am sorry in my heart to hear of any trouble."

"Don't you know already? The people's tongues go sharp enough just now."

"Oh, yes, I do understand: that bad man you mean, who make mischief everywhere! Did you hear anything new?"

" No ; only just now, you see, I met the fellow coming away from Clogwyn. I never see that without feeling some strange sort of thing come over me. The poor little girl there! indeed, I vex in my heart about her. If the father knew, I am sure he would break his heart. I see it very strange, Mrs. Parry let the people come to the house. I always tell that woman is not very strong in the head; she talk too much."

Hugh got up, then sank into his chair again and fell into a second reverie.

" Can't something be done to stop that man from going there ?" suggested his wife, who had no respect for Lord Morlif, and always designated him " that man."

" That's it!" exclaimed Hugh, in so loud a voice that his companion was startled. I would give this hand if I could only do that! Yes, indeed I would."

" Perhaps it could be done without that," replied his wife, smiling archly at his zeal.

"Tell me how, and I won't sleep till it is done."

"Why, go up to Clogwyn, and speak with the little girl yourself; tell her plain out, the father no like Lord Morlif, and he is a bad man."

"That would do—yes, indeed, that would do. Only I think, Molly, you had better go instead of me. It would be better to come from you. Yes, my little missus, you must go. Something tell me she would somehow be more comfortable like with you. I am so rough, you know. I should not either like to walk over those grand carpets without taking off my shoes; and perhaps that would not do, it would look odd. The little lady, perhaps, would not like it. Come, say, Molly, you will go; promise me that."

"Well, well — yes, if you, wish it: but you must tell me what to say."

"Oh yes, I will tell you what to say," said Hugh, rising once more hastily from his seat, and thrusting his hands into his pockets, while he grew red from excitement,—" I will tell you what to say :—tell her that if her father was here, and found that man in his house, he would shoot him, as he would shoot a partridge. That's what you must tell her."

" No, no, Hugh bach; I can't, indeed, speak to the young lady in that way. I should make a fear come over her."

" Well, then, what is to be done? It must be told to her, you see."

" Yes, yes, to be sure ; but not in that way. I will speak to Mrs. Parry, and ask her to break it to the young lady.".

" No, indeed, you not tell anybody but the little mistress herself. Mrs. Parry talk too much, she will only make mischief. Listen to what I am going to tell you ; you not hear before. This bad man Morlif is the Captain's greatest enemy! Tell her that! and that he make great harm for him some years ago; so that if her father live to be a hundred, he will never forgive him. Tell

c 2

her that; and you must make her see, in every way, it is an ugly thing—yes, a very ugly thing—for her to talk to the man at all, or let him come near her. Poor little thing! she does not know there is any harm in it, and nobody will tell her; so you see, Molly, *you* must tell her. Do you understand?"

"Yes, I understand, but don't talk so loud; don't be so hasty—we must think on it a little first, Hugh bach. Suppose she not like me to tell her—suppose what the people say is true—she like the man."

"Tut! nonsense! fie, fie! Do you think for a moment that pretty young thing, belonging to a man like Lewis, would take a fancy to that thin, yellow-faced man with those bad eyes, and with hands and a voice like a woman's? No, that is not possible. Besides, does she not care too much for the son of Bleddyn, to make friends with any other man? That's it, you see."

"Indeed, Hugh, I should be glad to do anything in my power to serve the daughter of Clogwyn; only I am afraid you talk with too much confidence. How can you tell if she really cares for the son of Bleddyn?"

"Because I know it, that it is so; and I see something in her that tells me she will some day be the mistress of the Plas—that's more."

"Dear me! I can remember the day you talked very differently."

"Well, I know that; but I did not know then all I do now: a man must speak as he finds things, not as things were."

"There may be truth in that. Do you think, then, there is a chance of Captain Lewis becoming friends with our landlord?"

"No, never, never!" Again Hugh's hands disappeared in his pockets.

"What is it you mean, then?"

"That I am not going to tell: you women talk so much, it is better not. But you may know this far, that there is not a tenant on the Bleddyn estate, not a poor man in the whole county, who would raise his hand to throw a stone at the heir of the Plas: no, not even if he were paid for it. That I know to be true; and it is saying a great deal in a few words, for a young gentleman, the son of that Owen Herbert who, through the Scotch agent, screws us down, so that we poor fellows are obliged to starve before we can pay our rents."

Hugh Lloyd was waxing warm, and his wife grew fidgety. She knew he was coming into the neighbourhood of a sore subject. Hugh continued—

" Let any one go into my yard, and look over those new stables and pigsties and cow-houses, and make an estimate of what they cost me—of what they took out of the pocket of a poor man with a large family, and then ask him, when he hears what follows, if it is not a crying shame? The moment they were finished, that scurvy rascal, who has been sneaking too often about here, pops down upon me, and begins by chewing his words, and slanting his eyes, and fidgeting his elbows. At last he says, in that very foolish way of his — 'Mr. Gwynne, my friend, Mr. Gwynne has sent me to inform you that he intends raising your rent from the next quarter-day.' What do you call that? What, I ask, does justice call it? I am a poor man; but a poor man has his heart, and his tongue in his head, the same as the great folks, and so he will ask these questions, and give his opinion, that there are scores of poor fellows who have been transported for a less offence than what this Owen Herbert Gwynne is answerable for. Indeed, Molly, somehow these things come creeping often into my brain, and I see something altogether wrong in the world, something that wants being put to rights. I don't know how it is to be done, only I know it must be done, or we shall have a smash up some of these days, as you will see. Fair play—I say, fair play to everybody. It is a wicked thing to throw a net over an honest man who is striving to better himself, and pin him down till he has no legs to stand upon. It is a hard thing that we cannot live in our quiet way, without the great people step in upon us, and run away with our bread and butter, and then do no good with it after all, but throw it to the dogs. Let us alone! let us alone! that's my cry. If they can't do their poor neighbours good, let them keep away altogether."

"I say the same, Hugh; we were better off when they were away than when we have had them with us. All the village would agree with me. Just see those two families, the Morlifs and the Sands, they do no good even to the tradespeople. They get all they want, and then never pay. There are great complaints everywhere."

"The tradespeople are foolish to let them have the things without first paying for them. They know as well as I do, that there are sharpers among the grand folks as well as in our class. They know what to expect. It is their own fault: I have told them so heaps of times."

"It looks very odd, when the great gentlemen have money, and yet not pay."

"It is more odd still when they don't know what to do with their money, that they can drain the last farthing out of the tenant's pocket."

"I don't know, but I think, if I were the landlord, and the landlord was my tenant, I would not treat him as he has treated me; nor do I think the young son of Bleddyn would either. O'r anwyl! if I were to wish for anything more than another, it would be to see that young man in the place of his father."

"Indeed, Hugh, it is odd, you have lately taken a great fancy to the young man."

"Well, yes: have not I seen some little things in him which speak good? I like him; and if I speak from my own heart, I should like to see him take his wife from the Clogwyn. He would have her from a good school — in a great house, that is everything. It would be the saving of Angharad. The little town is going to pieces as fast as it can. One bad man brings another, till we have a nest-full. There was such a row last night at the lower end of the village! You never hear nor see such things. There was that young Morlif, and those two wild young men the Sands, with another fellow worse than all of them put together, kicking up such a noise you never heard the like. Then they were making the fellows drunk, and doing what young gentlemen ought not to have been doing. Never, since I can remember this little place, did I see such things as I was witness to last night. Had it not been for Mr. Cad Maurice and his cousin, I believe they would have set fire to the houses, and have done no end of damage. I really don't think they know what they were about. It was a disgrace, a shame! They wanted

Captain Lewis there: he would soon have put a stop to it, I know. I can see there is a great change ever since he left; nobody knows what weight he had with all the people. Why is this, my little missus? Because he is just. I wish, poor fellow, Australia had been drowned in the sea, before he left us to go there! But, dear me! here comes Will Thomas and Ellis. We have been losing time; go, now, and put your bonnet on, and try and get to Clogwyn before it is dark. I cannot rest till I know you have opened poor Miss Lewis's eyes. Come, my little woman."

"Not to-night, Hugh; it is late."

"Yes, yes, to-night; it does not rain now, and there is plenty of time. You will perhaps not have time to go to morrow, or she may be out: better indeed go now, and Robin can go with you to bring you back."

Hugh could not conceal his impatience. His wife knew, from long experience, there was no use parleying the point when anybody's interest was in view; so she put up her knitting, and went to adorn herself in her Sunday dress, a maroon linsey-woolsey, a black stuff apron, a shawl, and a close bonnet. These were soon neatly arranged upon her dapper person, and with a pair of brightly-polished shoes, tied with a great bunch of riband, she issued from under the old sign in company with her son. This son had rushed into manhood so hastily, that he was more than head and shoulders above his mother, and promised to be a fine young man. He had long wished to go to Clogwyn, if it were only to see the grand kitchen which everybody talked about. At the prospect of his wishes being realized, he was in good spirits, and his mother found him excellent company.

Hugh was now left to entertain the guests. He had never felt such a disinclination to fulfil that office. He could scarcely get through his pipe, and scarcely touched his beer. He almost wished he had gone with his wife in place of his son; but it was too late now; he must content himself to wait until their return.

When they had been gone considerably above an hour, Hugh got up, left the house, and strolled a long way up the road to see if he could observe any signs of their coming. The dogs were barking at the other end of the town, and perhaps there was another row going on. Where he stood, all was quiet; he could neither hear nor see anything—not even a leaf was stirring. He soon retraced his steps, and stood in his kitchen before the old clock. It had struck ten: what could make them so late? Again the hand was going round, and had made some considerable strides towards eleven, when he caught the welcome sound of voices at last.

In came the little woman, looking warm, but with a beaming expression of countenance, so that Hugh, without asking the question, knew at once her mission had met with success.

"Dear anwyl! we have had a long walk; Clogwyn is much further off than I thought it was," said she, disencumbering herself of her bonnet and shawl, and sitting upon the settle. "I am quite tired."

"Mother ought not to be," said the lad, "for we had a long rest, and such a supper as I never saw, nor never made before. Father, you don't know what a grand place it is; and all the people so civil!"

"And so fine, so comfortable, and so clean!" broke in the mother; "and the people tell stories when they say the daughter of Clogwyn is proud. She is not a bit proud, Hugh—not at all like those people who come from Liverpool, and drive in that blue carriage. They are not ladies, and are proud. Miss Lewis is a lady all over, and no proud un t'all. Oh, she is so nice, so quiet, and with such pretty hair! I never see nobody like her. Then she was so kind to me!—she make me sit down in such a grand chair; but it was very low, and so soft that I did not know where I was going to: and, indeed, when I first went into that grand room, with large pictures in gold frames, and marble figures, and such lots of pretty things, really, Hugh bach, I began to be frightened. But, somehow, the moment she come and spoke to me, it all went away. Was not that curious? Poor little thing! indeed I am sorry for her. She look sad in the face, and I am sure she feel her father go away very much. Pity, pity, she got no mother. Mrs. Parry is no fit for a nice lady like that: no, no, indeed."

"Well, tell me, did you tell her what I told you?" asked Hugh, impatiently.

"Oh yes, by degrees; and she no look offended, only she turn white, and I see her poor little hands tremble. She give me her hand before I go away, and thank me kindly. Oh, she is a nice lady; such a nice face! Poor little thing! and she got no mother."

" But will she do it ?"

" Do what ?"

" Why, keep that man from coming to the house."

" To be sure she will. She tell me, with a very serious face, that she wished I had told her that before, and he should never have put his foot in the house. She does not like him at all, I am sure; so you were right, Hugh, and the people no tell the truth."

" Well, I am glad ; I can go to bed now, and sleep soundly till the morning."

There was an unmistakeable look of pleasure and satisfaction in Hugh's physiognomy, but he was very absent. Instead of saluting his daughter in wishing her good-night, he kissed his long-legged son, not the least aware of what he had done till he heard some tittering behind his back.

" Come, come, my little woman, now let us all go to bed, and be thankful we have done a kind act to-day to a neighbour."

CHAPTER III.

The yellow leaves are falling, and whirling in the air; and the wintry winds have already begun to howl and sweep drearily round the high gables of Clogwyn. The general aspect is cold and cheerless. But where is she, the young mistress of the mansion? Not in the library, nor upon the terrace, nor in the garden. She is in the drawing-room, seated upon a low chair, dressed in deep mourning, and looking pale and dejected. Lady Elizabeth has been announced, and a warm greeting has just taken place.

"My solitary little Gertrude, I am so

distressed for you!" said Lady Elizabeth, holding her in her arms. "It is sad for you to be alone in this great house. You must be lamenting your father's absence more than ever, my dear."

"Yes, I do. The house does feel lonely and still. Your absence, too, has made it all the more trying for me. But I have not been divested of sympathy among the poor. Their little attentions have been quite touching. The house at this moment is loaded with offerings—a curious custom, and a primitive way of showing respect. Poor Yarico, too, has been a great comfort to me. Between us, you know, there exists a species of affection undefinable."

"I do not know Yarico sufficiently to estimate her worth; but I am glad you have had some one to cheer you. It was so unfortunate that I was away! Anarawd will be distressed when he hears it; yet, we could not foresee these things."

"Oh no; and it is all over now. You

are going to spend the winter at Bleddyn; that will fully compensate for all I have lately gone through. To feel you are there will be a great comfort to me."

" I was pleased to hear Mr. Maurice has been a good friend to you in your trouble."

" I do not know what I should have done without him. I sent for him and the doctor the moment poor Mrs. Parry was seized. She was gone before they arrived."

" A dreadful shock for you, my poor Gertrude!"

" Oh yes, a terrible shock; I shan't get over it for some time."

" Change of scene s the only cure. I have come purposely to take you back with me to Bleddyn. I am alone there, and shall be delighted to have your company."

" It would be charming; but I don't know what to say to your proposal: perhaps papa would not like my leaving home."

" He could not object: you will be safer with me, than here unprotected and alone."

"The answer which rushes up from my heart says I am too glad to come: it will be a relief to get away from here for a time."

"Ring, then, for Yarico, and order her to put up your things. My invitation, of course, extends to your faithful negress."

"How kind! I am always so happy with you!" Her face brightened; she rang the bell, and gave the necessary orders.

While the preparations were making, they continued in conversation.

Had she heard from her father? Lady Elizabeth inquired.

"No: I am extremely anxious about him. To be separated from him and Anarawd has been a bitter trial; in your absence, unbearable—you cannot imagine how rejoiced I am to have you back."

While she spoke, her sad eyes grew earnest, and the hand she held was pressed warmly between her own. There was that natural, genuine warmth in Gertrude's manner which particularly endeared her to Lady Elizabeth. Absence seemed to have tightened the cords of friendship. It was a reaction of enjoyment to be again in each other's society.

After a pause, Gertrude resumed—

"I can hardly realize poor Mrs. Parry's loss. Though she was not a congenial companion, I do somehow miss her, and see her virtues more than I did when she was alive. I regret sorely now that I was so unamiable in my bearing towards her. I have unfortunately such an innate dislike to noisy, coarse-minded people, that I know my temper was constantly ruffled when it ought not have been. The truth is, dear Lady Elizabeth, I am not amiable."

"I would not judge you so harshly. Human nature will unveil itself, taking varied forms. When you see you have committed a fault, do not repine over it, but take a lesson from it for the future. Were we to investigate closely, I am afraid we all more or less are too regardful of the minor imperfections of those with whom we are destined to associate, instead of estimating their characters on an extensive scale as a whole. Poor weak human nature is sadly defective! It is as hard to govern our antipathies as it is to control our affections;—hard to submit to the curb to prevent us from running into extremes. Checkered as the world is with imperfections, we do indeed stand in need of the charity which St. Paul preaches. Could the hearts of mankind be generally unmasked, I fear that the best of us would be little better than our neighbours. Let us, then, wear the garment of charity: that will keep up the right degree of warmth about the heart, and act as a shield to protect it from the many and daily evils which trammel our path in life, and make it wretched."

That evening Gertrude found herself sitting upon the hearth at Bleddyn, enjoying the peaceful twilight, before a blazing fire.

At the further end of the room hung a full-length portrait of young Gwynne, and by the fire reflected upon the canvas the features were clearly exhibited. Gertrude's eye wandered continually in that direction. She was more silent than usual. His name was often in her thoughts, and she longed to make him the subject of conversation, but required courage to do it.

"It is very like him!" said Lady Elizabeth, in a quiet, absent manner, as she followed her young companion's eye in the direction of the picture.

Gertrude started; she felt her thoughts had been read.

"My dear Anarawd! what would he give, Gertrude, to be our companion at this moment? When he left, how little prepared we were for this prolonged separation! With all my endeavours, I can get no direct answer from Mr. Gwynne as to when we may expect him home. I have a suspicion that it is his intention to keep Anarawd at the University of Heidelberg, to complete his military education there, instead of finishing his studies at Oxford. My suspicion may prove erroneous; I hope it may, for in that case, we should not see him for some months longer. How could I support it, Gertrude? Already I have felt the separation keenly."

Gertrude's heart shrunk within her, as a deep-drawn sigh accompanied the words, and her gaze became instantly riveted upon Lady Elizabeth's face. She was leaning back in her arm-chair, and her eyes closed. A solitary tear rolled down her cheek, and fell upon the handkerchief which lay upon her lap. There was a long silence, for both were struggling with their feelings. Gertrude's excitement increased; the sensation in her temples grew to a heavy throb, and the misgivings at her heart oppressed her. At last, losing all control over herself, she rose abruptly, and the next instant sank down upon an ottoman before her friend, exclaiming, with tears in her eyes—

" How is it, dear Lady Elizabeth, how is it you treat me with so much kindness—with such gentleness and forbearance, with so much sympathy—when I must be the cause of this separation between mother and son? I have brought heavy trouble and misery on you both. Why is it you do not act as others would,—hate me—banish me from your society—spurn me—upbraid me?"

Lady Elizabeth put her hand upon her head. "Hush, Gertrude: if you do not wish to cause me pain, do not speak in this excited manner; be calm, and listen to reason. Supposing my sorrow originates with you, there can be no blame attached; you are innocently the cause; and would it not be unnatural in a mother to upbraid and treat unkindly one to whom her son is so deeply and devotedly attached? The world, I am aware, unsparingly condemns me for the part I have taken. The world is not a fit judge between mother and son. A mother's eye can penetrate beyond what comes under the world's vulgar observation. Does not her pure, disinterested love point out intuitively the most direct path by which happiness may be secured? I have seen and experienced enough of life to know that the evils accruing from ill-assorted unions have ever cankered and withered the heart. The aim of every mother should be to prevent so sad a catastrophe. Hitherto we have spoken little upon this subject, my dear Gertrude: now you are with me, we shall have frequent opportunities of renewing that which interests us both so deeply. The world, as I before observed, censures me for the part I have taken; but, knowing Anarawd's disposition as I do, I could not acquiesce with his father and friends in supposing his attachment to you to be a mere boyish fancy, and the quicker the engagement was broken off the better. He is young, I am ready to admit, and had he been one of an ordinary character and of a susceptible nature, and my Gertrude as impulsive and unreasonable as she is sometimes in words, perhaps I should not have been so unyielding, but have conformed and seconded his father's views. This happens not to be the case, as we know, my dear Gertrude. From early childhood have I not made my son's disposition my peculiar study, and watched over him with maternal solicitude? Have I not long since discovered that singular steadfastness of character—that deep, earnest affection which has taken root in him from early childhood, and has become a part of his nature? There is no changeableness in his character—none whatever. I feel I cannot tamper with a nature such as his, or mistrust his judgment. When he tells me, Gertrude, you are the only woman in the world he could ever love, the only being calculated to make him happy and share his destiny, I believe him. I may not live to see the day when you are united; but when that period does arrive, those who see it will be ready to own I was not in error when I promoted that which was strongly opposed to his father's worldly views. Now a few words exclusively to yourself. I have not been with you so long without discovering, independently of my son's testimony, that you are calculated to fulfil the mission of a wife, a wife suitable to Anarawd. With you I feel he would be happy, and there would be no fear of your undervaluing his affection. As regards my own feelings, I know none—none, my dear child, whom I desire for a daughter so earnestly as I do you, my little friend and cheerful companion. Already I feel you are my child, and you will ever continue to be so, will you not? You will promise to make my dear boy a good and affectionate wife, the greatest blessing a man can have. In return you will be cherished, and not forsaken by him. Bless you, dear child! without a reply, I can see you will do all that is required of you, and more."

"God grant it!" murmured Gertrude, her heart too full to give further utterance to her feelings. How great the regard she felt, how powerful the motive to love Lady Elizabeth at that moment, and how earnestly she longed for the absent to be present, cannot be described.

"You are not so strong as you were, I perceive, my dear Gertrude: I have overexcited you. We must banish the subject for a time. Try and compose yourself."

The fire crackled cheerfully upon the hearth; twilight had lapsed into night, and the gusts of wind occasionally drove a shower of leaves against the window-panes, then rushed away again, and fresh cracklings were heard among the naked boughs of the elm upon the lawn.

"What a wild-sounding night it is!" said Lady Elizabeth. "It makes us all the more appreciate the comforts of our fireside. There is a dreamy feeling about firelight; something highly composing."

"Yes, I love firelight," repeated Gertrude, rousing herself from a pleasant reverie.

"And here comes a footstep to put an end to the charm," said Lady Elizabeth. The door opened.

"Lord Morlif is in the library," said the footman, advancing to the centre of the room. "He wishes to speak to your ladyship."

"Tell him I am sorry I cannot see him this evening. I don't feel well. I am not equal to it."

"His lordship desired me to say he would not detain you many minutes."

"I cannot—indeed, Jones, I cannot see him to-night. You must make an apology for me."

The servant lingered as if he partly expected his mistress would change her mind; but she was unbending, actuated, probably, by all-sufficing motives.

At the moment Lord Morlif's name was mentioned, Gertrude started up as if she had received an electric shock, and hurried across the room to one of the window recesses, where she stood looking out on the moonlight scene, in fear lest Lady Elizabeth should admit his lordship. A few moments before, she was in a happy reverie; now, her thoughts were painfully disturbed. Her persecutor was in the same house with her, and a partition only separated them.

They had met Lord Morlif that same afternoon, as they drove from Clogwyn to Bleddyn. What could have brought him out that windy night, unless it was to continue such distasteful and pointed attentions as he had been accustomed to exhibit whenever she had come to Bleddyn? She had had a respite for a few weeks; but now she seemed to be in danger of having the pleasure of her visit marred by him, unless she disclosed to Lady Elizabeth all that had taken place since Anarawd left, and entreated her to be her protectress. She had the opportunity now; and the sooner her statement was made, the better. Lady Elizabeth should know what an unprincipled man he was, and what advantage he had taken of her unprotected position. She felt a deep revulsion on the mention of his name, being convinced that an honourable, upright, spirited man would crush such a contemptible personage as he was under foot, could he know of his lordship's baseness. She only regretted that she had not discovered in the first instance his dissolute character,—that his moralizing was base hypocrisy, and his pretended philosophy wretched sophistry. Not one good point attached to him, in disposition, nature, or acquirement. He had spoken to her in a manner wholly indefensible, even under the hollow sanction of fashionable life. She felt conscious of his repeated insults of this kind, which it pained her to recall. If the world was as wicked as he affected to represent it, there was no happiness in being made acquainted with it. She was much happier in her ignorance. She could not disclose to Lady Elizabeth all his insinuations, all he had said to her—it was impossible; while her ladyship might wonder she had not before told her, giving her conduct the air of concealment. Many things had been said by his lordship which had made her exceedingly uncomfortable, so much so as to depress her spirits. What he had stated about her father was mortifying, supposing it was untrue. She felt convinced that what his lordship had communicated was not the fact. Truth was no part of his nature.

She put her face close to the window-pane, and again looked out upon the wild, void night. She asked herself again and again, why her heart beat in that way— why she should be so frightened, whenever she knew Lord Morlif to be near. She wondered if there were many such bad men in the world as he was; and if so, how sad it was to be living in such a wicked world, where society countenanced such individuals. Such was the simplicity of Gertrude's character, and her slight acquaintance with the run of society. To be thrown into Lord Morlif's presence, and to be obliged to listen to him, had already been sufficiently annoying and harassing to her feelings. Anarawd and her father would be indignant and angry to hear what she had to reveal to them. She was determined, notwithstanding, to hide nothing from them, even if she were herself to blame in the matter.

With a nervous footstep she turned from the window, and observed that lights had been brought in, and that Lady Elizabeth appeared inclined to doze. When the tea-things were placed upon the table, she roused herself and requested Gertrude to preside.

Readily complying, the latter took her place at the tray, when both relapsed into silence. Gertrude began to recall to herself the many happy evenings she had spent in that room: how often had Anarawd sat close to her upon a particular chair which was now empty!—his kind way with his mother, his content with his home, his consideration for the servants, and that pleasant, cheerful manner he always carried: Oh, how she longed to see him there once more! Her thoughts, too, again reverted to Lord Morlif. She had not yet heard the opening and shutting of the hall-door. Perhaps he was not yet gone; what could have made him stay? He was discolouring everything in her view, checking her happier thoughts. She nearly tossed her cup over as the door suddenly opened, and looked up as if under the apprehension of seeing Lord Morlif. It was only the footman, who handed her two letters. Upon the envelope of one, she recognized Mr. Gwynne's writing, addressed to Lord Morlif. The other was addressed to herself; she knew but too well from whom it came.

"What! is his lordship still here?" said Lady Elizabeth, looking up in surprise as Gertrude handed over the letter intended for her.

"Yes, my lady; but he is putting on his coat, and will leave directly."

"I hope Williams is attending to him?"

"Yes, my lady."

"What sort of night is it? If it is raining, he had better have the carriage."

"Oh no, my lady, it is not raining; the moon is up—it is quite fine."

"Has his lordship been in the library all this time?"

"Yes, my lady."

"The fire, I hope, had not gone out?"

"No, my lady, it has been attended to."

Not a word of this was heard by Gertrude. Her eyes rested upon the letter she had just received. She was determined Lady Elizabeth should read it. She would not burn it, as she had done with his lordship's previous letters. The letter would show her friend what Lord Morlif was, better than she could explain.

She felt impatient for the servant to take away the tea-things, and Lady Elizabeth seemed as if she never would finish her last cup. Even the large favourite tortoiseshell cat lapped her milk too lazily for Gertrude's patience.

The things removed, Gertrude stood up facing her friend. The shutting of the front door, and the bars drawn at the same instant, caught her ear. Lord Morlif was, then, really gone. She was deeply thankful.

"Gertrude, my dear, what is the reason you appear so restless and nervous? Why that distressed look and flushed cheek? Something unusual has occurred—what is it, dear?"

"I have one peculiar annoyance," replied Gertrude, "one which distresses me greatly."

"That I do not know of?"

"Yes, my dear Lady Elizabeth, I have much to tell you that will grieve you. It has been preying upon my mind a long while."

She drew one of the low chairs close to Lady Elizabeth, and seating herself, the latter said—

"Well, what is it?"

"You are aware, dear Lady Elizabeth, you have been away from home a great deal since Anarawd left,—once into Denbighshire, and with your friends at Barmouth. Thus I have had no opportunity of talking to you about my own affairs. I could not well communicate by letter what I desired to say, because it requires so much explanation. I have kept it from you till now."

Gertrude looked nervous and confused.

"My dear child, what has happened?"

"Ever since Anarawd left, Lord Morlif has been daily annoying me by his attentions. All the time you have been away, I have been in a most unpleasant situation."

"Gertrude, you alarm me! His lordship is a most intriguing, dangerous character, not fit for the companionship of any young person. I am grieved: I warned you, Gertrude, and hoped you would avoid him."

"I have done all in my power, Lady Elizabeth, to keep free of his presence," replied Gertrude, bursting into tears at her friend's unaccustomed severity of manner. It was through other people, not myself, that I was thrown into his company. Mrs. Parry encouraged him. I wonder, too, you have not observed that Mr. Gwynne has invariably placed me in his way. No one can tell what I have had to endure from his persecution! He has said all sorts of disgraceful things to me; I should not like—indeed, I could not repeat them. I loathe and detest him!"

"Oh! Gertrude, you have acted most unwisely and wrongly; why did you not tell me of it in the first instance? I had not the slightest suspicion of anything of that nature."

"I did not know what his intentions

were at first. It would have seemed vanity in me to have spoken for what might have been no more than social usage to our sex. I am deeply grieved to have done anything you consider wrong. I am certain, could you know the circumstances from beginning to end, you would not say I am much to blame."

"Well, my dear child, do not weep in this distressing way. What has been done cannot be undone. We must prevent any further persecution from Lord Morlif. Perhaps I deserve greater censure than yourself, for not looking more vigilantly after my charge. Poor Anarawd! he will feel my neglect keenly; I deserve his reproach."

Oh no, dear Lady Elizabeth: if any one merits his censure, it is myself, and I will take the blame." She paused, then continued—

"I have written frequently to Anarawd, and concealed nothing from him. If I could only be sure of his getting those letters before this cruel, unauthorized report of my going to be married to Lord Morlif reaches him, all will yet be well. But the chance is, in his wanderings those letters may never come into his possession for weeks hence. It is this uncertainty which makes me miserable."

"It is singular I should never have heard of these reports."

"You were not at Bleddyn when they began to be circulated. I have a strong suspicion that Lord Morlif himself spread the false report in the neighbourhood. He is such a falsifier, there is nothing he would not do to suit his own evil purposes. He endeavours to make every one believe I am pleased with his attentions, when he knows from the first that I have always repulsed him. Candidly and positively, I can declare I have ever been wretched in his presence, and annoyed by his attentions; while his conversation has been most distasteful to me. Had I been older—had I had more experience—had I possessed more confidence and self-possession, things would not have been so painful. Unfortunately, he discovered my weak points, and took advantage of my inexperience. You best know, dear Lady Elizabeth, when a dissipated and artful man acts thus, how soon one like myself becomes bound in trammels. What one has to endure in silence, the indignant heart alone can express! I have been miserable indeed! While I am at Bleddyn, will you shield me? Will you never let me be alone in his company? And do not, dear Lady Elizabeth, look angry upon me, but protect me from that wicked man."

"I am not angry with you, dear; only grieved more than words can express. Come, kiss me, and let me not see you in this distress. I shall take every precaution you do not see him again."

"This is not all," sobbed Gertrude. "Lord Morlif, I have lately discovered, is my father's enemy, and he will be displeased indeed to hear of his being intimate at Clogwyn. What will he say when I acquaint him with what has happened? I dread his displeasure."

"It is an unfortunate affair: indeed, Gertrude, I shall never forgive myself for not having been more observant. I begin to see now Mr. Gwynne's motive for urging me to go into Denbighshire. Do not, my dear child, grieve about your father: the blame rests with me. I shall tell him so."

The characters which Gertrude's eye never traced, yet for whose glances they were intended, underwent a close scrutiny by Lady Elizabeth. On the commencement of the perusal, she looked serious, and as she read on she became nervous and agitated, and drew the candle nearer to her. Again and again she read over some of the passages, as if incredulous as to their real purport; but the characters were too clearly written for misinterpretation. When she had satisfied herself what the meaning was, she crushed the paper between her fingers, and committed it to the flames. " Unmitigated villain!" were the only words which escaped her lips.

CHAPTER IV.

A CUTTING wind had set in, sweeping direct from the far-off snows of the frozen north. The autumnal tints had lost their early and more varied richness, and, fading, had put on their brown, arid hue. The storks no longer sat reposing upon the house-tops of the old Teutonic city of Heidelberg. All looked sad and battered, not as it had appeared two months before, under the glow of a rosy sunset, such as is seldom seen anywhere in greater beauty than it is from the long walk in the grounds of the venerable castle. Heidelberg no longer seems the same place: every face there looks cold and shrivelled.

Children whimper along the streets, and mothers, apparently turning a deaf ear to their cries, hurry on to reach their homes; and to get out of the bleak, cutting wind, is the main object of everybody. It was Saturday, and all could not so easily find the comfort they needed when they did reach their homes. On this day of the week, houses, and even the pavement itself, had to submit to the operation of being washed down, or rather deluged with water. Wherever you turned, right or left, into Straszes or Gasses, it was the same—wet, comfortless, and sloppy! The busy operators, too much occupied to notice or regard the luckless passengers, constantly threatening them with a fresh pail of water close at their heels, sent them jostling against others, as ill-treated as themselves. Then came the ceaseless sound of the woodsawing everywhere around, and the unloading of the timber from the long light waggons, bullock-drawn, stopping up the thoroughfare at every turn. All indicated that winter was approaching, and preparations were making to meet its nipping blasts. Even now, the cutting wind drives every one onwards, not a soul lingers. The Haupt-strasze begins to thin, and the shop-doors are closed. This scantiness of population makes the sight of two gentlemen on the opposite side of the street more conspicuous. They would at once have been recognised as Englishmen, by their gait. Like the inhabitants, they too hurry on with rapid strides. When they arrive at the bottom of the Haupt-strasze, and are near the railway station, they enter into conversation.

"I don't like leaving you here, Gwynne; I am afraid you will pass a miserable winter, it is so horribly cold," said one of the Englishmen to his companion.

"I care little about the cold; if I were in England, I should be in Oxford, not at home. It is all the same thing, no matter."

"Don't speak so despondingly, my dear fellow. I should feel I left you in far greater comfort, if you keep to your old quarters at the hotel, instead of locating yourself in those miserable rooms in the court of the old castle. They are not fit to house a bat."

"I abominate an hotel, and a boarding-house is still worse. Leave me to go to my quarters in peace. I shall keep roaring fires; there is no lack of wood, and the stoves, you know, heat the room to suffocation if one desires it. Where can a Briton not live? In what realm, clime, or under what political state of government, is he not to be found, and grumbling everywhere?"

"Ha, ha! Well, Gwynne, you must have your own way. Write to me, and tell me how you are getting on. If you do get tired of your quarters, you can change them. You have my address for the next six weeks: after that time, any letters sent to the Union Club, London, will find me. Get on with your mathematics and German; you want to perfect yourself in little else; in fact, you are pretty well up in them. Still, we need never be afraid of learning too much. Your father does not seem to think you are doing so. Keep to it. Should you make acquaintances with any of these white-and-red cap gentlemen, take care you do not get into any rows with them. They are a set of fiery, wrong-headed, obstinate dogs, not worth an Englishman's showing them his fists."

"You need not be alarmed. I am not one of your over-sociable beings. If I cannot form a clique of my own, I prefer solitude. I am an Englishman all over, as the Germans would say. You will see my father, I suppose, when you get to England. I hear he is in town."

"Certainly, I shall call upon him immediately."

"When you write, let me know what passes between you. Don't omit telling him what I told you."

"No."

"I have a favour to ask you. Will you go

down to Bleddyn, if only for a few days? My mother would be delighted to see you. I know she would like to question you about me; it would comfort her. She writes in such low spirits. I am certain she is not happy at my being away. Will you go, Gilford,—will you?"

"If there is any good to be done, I shall be glad to oblige you."

"Thank you kindly. You will go, then: don't delay, nor describe my rooms; I would rather you did not. Tell my dear mother, I am as happy here, and as comfortable, as I should be were I at Oxford. Try and cheer her; pray do. Now, will you, Gilford? Write me, too, a long letter, when you get there. Tell me everything—how she is in health, and if she grieves much. There are a thousand things I should like to hear, and"—he hesitated—"and, Gertrude, you will not forget to tell me about her, everything—remember everything, that you know will interest me. Tell Gertrude, I cannot account for her silence, and if she knew how many times I have been to the post-office inquiring for an English letter, she would not, I am sure, treat me so cruelly. Letters increase in weight when they have been sprinkled with a little of the salt water which divides us from England; but none seem to be aware of this, save those who have had the experience."

"You should not fret about your letters. Ten chances to one whether half that have been sent from England have come to hand. Consider how constantly we have been on the move."

"Well, perhaps so. Yet, by this time, they must know where I am settled. Will you be able to go soon into Wales?"

"While in Shropshire, I can easily run down to Bleddyn, and will execute my mission as much to your satisfaction as possible. You may soon expect a sermon of a letter from me, such as you never had before; one which will rivet your attention, and keep you from thinking of mathematics for a week at least."

Anarawd laughed, and thanked him heartily. At the same moment they entered the railway station.

"There goes that horrid whistle; and I have not half thanked you, nor half told what I wished to say. I am sorry you are going, Gilford. I shall at first feel miserably dull; but I suppose I shall grow used to the life, as a monk does to his cell. Shall I get your ticket for you, while you look after your luggage? Why, if that booby is not taking it off to the other side! This is your train!"

Mr. Gilford rushed after his luggage in a fluster, while Anarawd strode composedly to the square hole and demanded a billet.

All was soon made straight. Mr. Gilford stepped into the carriage, and put his head out to give his friend his parting nod, and the parting words—"God bless you!"

There was a thickness about his voice, and some liquid glistened about his eyes, but Anarawd did not see it. The train was off, and he found himself standing alone upon the platform, without a single friend in a strange land; a position chilling indeed to those who are strangers to foreign travel on their first expedition.

It was nearly dark. Silently and solitarily he retraced his steps to his rooms in the castle court. He did not return by the Haupt-strasze, from the recollection of the saturated streets, but went immediately into the avenue, and so continued until he reached the precincts of the castle. A lonely feeling came over him, as he passed under the great gateway, more than usually gloomy as it was at that moment. In the large court, enclosed by the shattered walls, with their gaping windows, he stood for some time looking round. There was a ghostly appearance about the whole place, which excited his imagination, leading his thoughts into the past history of this magnificent ruined pile, when chivalry was rife, and mystery and superstition coloured all romance. The moon was struggling to disentangle herself from a thick drapery of white clouds; and those clouds seemed to approach and to rest upon the ruined walls, like messengers sent to look down upon him, and ask why he lingered there. It was but an optical illusion harmonizing with his thoughts, and seemed a token of unknown things to come.

As he gazed and gazed again, the partly-obscured luminary broke forth, the clouds disappeared, and the satellite was in full splendour. Can that be a prescient of the future with me, thought Anarawd? My life darkened now, will it ever in like manner break forth clear of clouds?"

Strolling from the court towards the noble terrace, his footfall was the only one to be heard. Not a living thing moved near, save an old owl, that fluttered lazily across the court and settled upon the ivied ruins. The wind, which had been so boisterous and aggravating throughout the day, had suddenly dropped with the parting sun, and all was calm. He stood for some time contemplating the scene before him. The Neckar flowed over its rocky bed and meandered in the plain below; the bridge and numerous small boats were reflected amid the moonshine; and lights were streaming from the houses on the opposite side, looking like descended stars. There, too, was the town, peaceful, reposing just beneath the shadow of the far-famed and ill-fated castle. All had a soothing effect upon his mind.

The numbness of his limbs at last aroused him from his reflections, and he sought the good people living in the corner of the court, to show him the way to his apartments.

A pretty-looking girl, with a lamp in her hand, walked before him across the court. He followed his conductress up a narrow stone staircase, and entered his strange abode. To him it indeed felt strange.

" And this is the place I have chosen for

my winter quarters?—my home!" said he to himself, dropping into a chair and glancing round the apartment. The stove had gone out, that cold cheerless night, and the lamp upon the table burned dimly. The boards looked comfortless, for there was only a slip of carpet on one side of the room; a meagre supply of chairs, two tables, and a sofa, comprised the whole furniture of which the apartment could boast, giving him anything but a cheerful greeting. A chill was upon his heart, in spite of all his efforts. He was mentally drawing a comparison between the discomforts before him, and his own bright home so far away, of which there were so many happy pictures present in his memory. His heart was there, and even his ear seemed straining for the sound of voices which had for him been so long silent. He became so lost in thought, that he did not hear the apologies the German attendant made for not having looked after the stove; and he was hardly aware he was watching her movements, as she stood raising a flame, and feeding with wood the ugly-looking receptacle. Meanwhile, too, she arranged the offensive spittoon, and pushed the table close to the high-backed sofa. She then drew out a white napkin, and laid it cornerways in the centre of the table. All this passed unobserved, until the sound of the crackling wood, and the streams of light issuing from the bottom of the stove, spread a genial warmth over the room, something like a welcome. He started up, and opened the lid of the roaring stove, and began to apostrophize the fire, that brought back cheerfulness to his heart. It almost reconciled him to the fire-worship of the Zoroastrians, so delightfully cheering was it at the moment.

The girl smiled as she saw the pleasure which the light of the fire brought into the young Englishman's face, and she asked him whether he would have supper or coffee: she could fetch him anything he wished from the *restaurant*.

"You may bring me coffee and some cold meat; that will be sufficient. Can't you let me have a better lamp than this? There are two things I cannot live without—good fires and abundance of light. Remember that I am likely to be here for some months, so it is as well you should know my wants."

With a graceful something between a little bow and a courtesy, she quitted the apartment, promising she would inquire about the lamp and do all in her power to make him contented; comfortable would be a word wrongly applied, for the word does not exist in the German territory or tongue, nor do the Germans comprehend its English meaning.

When the first solitary meal was over, and the door was closed and bolted for the night, Anarawd seated himself again in the shabby, quaint-looking arm-chair, the only bit of furniture which had the smallest pretension to comfort and snugness. He again, as before, began to cogitate. In fact, he could do nothing else. Had he been like most of the fast young Englishmen fresh from Oxford upon their Continental tours, he would have resorted to his cigar, kicked his portmanteau to the further end of the room, tossed the spittoon out of the window, sworn at it, and abused the whole race of Germans, from the time of Carlomagne to Leopold, for their disgusting habits; while he would scorn to reconcile himself to Continental modes of life. He would prefer setting his face dead against everything he encountered, and would have been fretting and storming about his room, at times tripping over the slip of carpet and muttering an oath. Such, and a number of minor miseries besides, are things of which his countrymen determine when abroad to manufacture giants, for the satisfaction of venting their spleen against them.

This was not Anarawd Gwynne's disposition, for he was a character far out of the common. Comfortless and uncongenial to him as that room and all that belonged to it might be, no similar demonstration of ill-will or complaint was ever shown. Thoughts such as follow did suggest themselves, perhaps, more than once. "This is not my country. These Germans are of a widely-different race from ourselves. I would not be a German in preference to a good old Briton; no, not to be the king of the Romans. Proud I have always been of my country; and coming here, and seeing how others live, increases that pride."

But, at the moment, Anarawd Gwynne was not thinking of the Germans, nor their country. His thoughts were too much engrossed with other matters of a more touching nature—the ties fron which his heart could not be unstrung. Dim as the light burned, there was light enough to perceive a glow upon his face, and that peculiar expansion of his eyes, natural to him, as he sat gazing upon the red glow emitted from the stove. In his mind's eye, Gertrude and his mother's images were prominent. "What would they think, could they but see him sitting there as he was at that instant in solitude? Once more he surveyed the room from corner to corner. "Oh! Gertrude, my darling, suppose I had not a better dwelling to offer you than this; would you still be ready to share my destiny? You told me you could face poverty and be happy anywhere with me. You spoke, I fear, without having a conception of what discomfort accompanies poverty. Yet, with some experience, I can respond, I could be happy anywhere with you, even here, were your eyes but upon me. It would be a palace, a cheerful home to me. How strange it is, that one individual should, in this mode, hold in keeping the happiness or misery of another! How singular the influence operating upon those minds, once strange to each other and now united, so admirably expressed in those German lines!—

> 'Zwei Seelen und ein Gedanke,
> Zwei Herzen und ein Schlag.'

Nature has so ordered it. Ah! then how

melancholy it is that any two similar minds should separate or change!"

"Yet," he said to himself, "many do fall apart, do change. What am I thinking about? why did the word 'change' ring in my ear? Can Gertrude change, with the strong proof I have had of her affection?—impossible!"

The word "change" continued to haunt his mind, that seemed bent upon mischief, suggesting all sorts of embarrassing questions. "Why was Gertrude silent? Too often, absence was known to cool affection: she was most attractive, and greatly admired. With all his warnings to her, and her own self-reliance, another might take his place. Gertrude was but a woman, after all; and many of her sex have forgotten, and will continue to forget, the absent lover. No one could have a high opinion of the world; it was a world of profession, more than action; Gertrude might be one of the worldly—she might forget him."

Such thoughts soon made him angry with himself. He had been dreaming; he was ungenerous, untrusting; he was wronging his gentle, loving Gertrude, she whose eyes he could see now before him, beaming with affection, as they did, when she repeated— " You have yet to learn how deeply a woman can love."

" There must be something here, some evil influence—Faust, perhaps—to make me wander in this way. Why should those heart-killing words fret and torment me? Banish them —yes, banish distrust from Gertrude's vocabulary and mine—obliterate them !"

He rose from his chair, as if glad that the stove required a supply of wood. It gave him occupation. Once up, he felt no inclination to go back into the seat; and he wandered about, looking into the bed-room to discover if there was anything like comfort there. An eider-down covering upon the bed promised to be warm; and an odd-looking wardrobe, or chest of drawers, with an escritoire, would be serviceable. Yes, he would endeavour to make the best of things as they stood—such was his conclusion.

"Dear old Gilford, I am sorry you are gone! I believe, after all, you know me better than I do myself. In one thing I will follow your advice: I will work my brain, and be ready to compete with others wherever destiny throws me. Knowledge brings strength of mind and power of hand. Since I am to be a poor man, I shall require it all the more. To throw me out of my inheritance, after all, may prove of service to me; without being clogged with riches, I shall be able to fly higher, be more vigorous of mind, more enterprising, more of a man in the true sense of the word, and be able to look at the world as it stands, and face it in storm and tempest. Are riches in the long-run to be envied? How few who possess them, out of the many, do what they ought! They know not the use of their wealth when they have it, and disregard its responsibilities. Man is inclined to be idle and wasteful, when he obtains wealth by the accident of birth; but when he obtains it by traffic or toil, he is never satisfied without continual augmentation. If he sits in the lap of plenty, it requires a strong stimulus to rouse him to a sense of justice to his own intellect; he often grows selfish without being aware of it, pampers his body and indulges his appetites, the greatest clog of all to intellect, without considering the injury he is doing himself, or reflecting on the good he has the power to do to others. To possess a fortune and spend it for the good of those who have a claim upon the possessors — to feel that many are benefited by your hand, that you are living for some great end, and not for self-interest alone; then, of all things, riches are most to be desired, most to be envied, while least abused. Here I feel my heart again fail me, and my resolution to submit to my father's edict weakens and almost vanishes. Suppose I live to see the day when Bleddyn passes from me into other hands; for in all probability I shall have to lease it when it comes to me, and the latent hopes treasured up from childhood, and the well-digested theories for improvements at Angharad, will be dashed to pieces by the conduct of an unjust father! You, my Gertrude, shall never know the sacrifice I am making; it shall never find utterance in words It is not for the lost wealth nor for the position I shall grieve, but for what wealth and position can do, and for the old walls of Bleddyn themselves. Deeply as I love you, my darling Gertrude, and all in all as you are to me, I dread to meet that day when I shall see a stranger in my place ruling over the little town of Angharad."

Thus he soliloquized, standing by the window looking into the castle court, his head leaning upon his hand, and these thoughts crowding into his mind. Suddenly he felt weariness, and observing that the stove was nearly out, he at once hurried to bed.

The following day was dark and gloomy, the sky almost rivalling the leaden atmosphere of London, and, to render it more like, a heavy mist hung upon the hills. As the day rose and the fog increased, the castle and the town of Heidelberg were both enveloped in its denseness. It had rained all night, and when Anarawd left his apartments to find his way to the English church, the castle court was wet and sloppy, dead leaves stopped up the gutters, and rotten sticks and boughs of trees were scattered everywhere around, the effect of the boisterous wind that had blown in the night. The prospect was dreary, yet hope sprung up in Anarawd's heart that the post might bring the long-looked-for and long-desired letter. He descended the hill, and reached the church-door in the rain without having given it a thought.

From the church he lost no time in proceeding to the post-office. Standing face to face with the government official, he asked the old question, if there was any English letter for " A. Gwynne, Esq."

With a smile, the man took up a pile of letters, and said he was not sure, but he thought he had one for him.

Anarawd could scarcely conceal his impatience, as he watched the official slowly turn over the letters one after the other, till he came to the last—there was none !

" Letters were lost; it must be so, he was sure of it. Did the postman think there was any possibility of recovering letters from Geneva, Baden Baden, or any other town ? It was probable some were lying there. He would give him that," he continued, producing a napoleon, " if he would only restore him the letters which he was convinced had been sent from England."

The man looked at the coin, then at his interrogator, with astonishment. " Did the young gentleman know the foreign monies? —that was a large sum."

" Yes, he knew the foreign coinage perfectly, and was welcome to that, if he would but produce the letters."

In a few minutes the full address was taken, and the tightly-buttoned-up official, bowing most respectfully, told him he might rely upon the letters being recovered should any be at the post-towns he had named. He chuckled within himself, and thought what fools Englishmen were thus to throw away their money.

Struggling against the disappointment, Anarawd was once more threading his way, in the midst of rain and fog, along the Haupt-strasze, feeling more cheerless and more solitary than before; yet he still bore up with a stout heart.

CHAPTER V.

LEAVING Germany for Bleddyn. The candles were burning low in their sockets; the red-hot cinder fire was dwindling gradually away, and Gertrude had been long gone to bed; still Lady Elizabeth sat musing. She could not get Gertrude's confession and Lord Morlif's letter out of her head, nor in any degree compose her mind. His baseness was unparalleled. She could not entirely see his aim; but that he had been at work, trying to undermine Gertrude's principles, and to shake the palladium of her faith, was too clear. When he had succeeded there, which perhaps he might have done, God only knew what his further intentions might be. She shuddered. Poor Gertrude! and that she herself should never have suspected anything wrong was going on! How blind she was in all those matters! Lord Morlif had no doubt been on his guard, as he always was in her presence. Her own absence, too, for so many weeks: all this was unfortunate. To the day of her death she should never cease to reproach herself. Anarawd would not censure her, but how deeply would he feel it!

The lady's-maid came at last, gliding into the room to see after her mistress. Begging her pardon, she thought something must be the matter: it was very late.

"Late as it is, Morgan, I have a letter to write before I go to bed; make up a good fire in my room. There will be no occasion for you to sit up. I can manage to-night without you."

Wistfully looking at her mistress a second time, Margaret Morgan left the room to do as she had been desired.

"Poor mistress! how ill she looks! I am sure something is the matter. Miss Lewis, when she came up to bed, was looking as white as a sheet, and her eyes red with crying. Dear me! I never see such a world as it is. When master is at home, there is no peace in the house; and when he is away, some fresh trouble comes. I wish from my heart Master Anarawd would come back from that nasty country, with no one for his companions but those ugly great-whiskered men. If he knew how missus felt and fretted since he left, nothing, I am sure, would keep him; he would make haste back. If it is true what the people in the country say, that master keeps him away on purpose to vex poor missus, master must have a black heart. It is a shame on him to treat his nice kind wife in that way; but—have I not said long ago?—he does not deserve her—she is a hundred times too good for him. Though he is my master, I can't bear him. I wish, indeed, he had a wife who would beat him, and scratch him, and teach him how to behave himself. He does not always know how to behave even in his own house. I pity my missus; I am sorry for her. Many the world call gentlemen that are not so—coarse and rude, and good for nothing!"

Having given vent to her thoughts, partly to herself and partly to the fire, Margaret rose from her knees, took up her light, and went shivering down the long passage to her chamber.

A short time afterwards, Lady Elizabeth quitted the drawing-room. Though the wind was whistling loud without, all within was noiseless. She, too, shivered as she passed through the great hall and ascended the fine old-fashioned carved oak staircase. She was glad to find a bright fire to cheer her when she reached her own room. Taking off her dress, she robed herself in a warm dressing-gown, and sat down to her escritoire, which her maid had placed close to the fire.

Full of indignation as she was, and determined on letting Lord Morlif know her feelings and strong resentment, while the pen was in her hand, she hesitated. "Perhaps, after all, it was better not to put them down on paper. Lord Morlif was a clever, deep, designing man, as she knew from past experience. For poor Gertrude's sake, it was necessary to be cautious. Would it not be more prudent to see him, and express herself orally? She would let him know how Englishwomen felt at outrages such as he contemplated, and how they could resent an insult. Even if it were not direct, how they despised intrigue and falsehood; and, above all, how unsparing they felt it their duty to be, in the condemnation of the opposite sex, for ruthlessly taking advantage of unsuspecting youth and innocence! How, in every case, it was to be resented and reprobated!"

She, therefore, wrote only a few lines, requesting Lord Morlif would call at Bleddyn, as she had something of importance to communicate. The note, she resolved, should go the first thing in the morning: the quicker the affair was settled the better, for she could not rest while matters stood as they were.

When Lady Elizabeth and Gertrude met at breakfast, neither of them looked refreshed. Lady Elizabeth spoke with more than usual kindness to Gertrude, wishing to prevent her from seeing how depressed in spirits she was herself.

"I think this morning would be nicely passed in arranging those ferns. What do you say, my dear Gertrude?" said she, the instant the breakfast things were removed. "You made such a pretty design with the maiden-hair fern the last time, that I am desirous you should help me again, if not with your little fingers, with your taste."

Gertrude readily complied, and they were soon poring over large books full of blotting-paper, writing out botanical names, and cutting out bits of paper to fasten down the stalks. In completing one of the pages, and turning over the leaf, Lady Elizabeth said, in a low voice —

"Gertrude, my dear, I have written to request Lord Morlif to call here to-day, but have given Jones orders to show him into the library. There is no fear of your encountering him."

"Thank you," murmured Gertrude. "I am afraid he will ask to see me. I dread his coming."

"Very likely, my dear, but his desire shall not be gratified. There he is, no doubt!" continued Lady Elizabeth, as a thundering rat-tat-tat-tat came upon the hall-door.

Gertrude, in a state of nervousness, was startled, and dropped the ferns she held in her hand upon the carpet. Lady Elizabeth, equally discomposed, walked about the room.

"Oh, dear! how I wish this interview was over, and his lordship out of the country! It is useless regretting the past, that I know; yet, Gertrude, my dear, I do regret your having permitted this affair to go on without my knowledge."

Gertrude sat motionless in her chair, looking the picture of misery. She was just saying something in reply to Lady Elizabeth, when the door opened, and, to the astonishment of both, Lord Morlif was announced in person.

Lady Elizabeth bowed haughtily, and, unable to conceal her indignation and annoyance, turned round and said to the servant—

"Jones, how is this? I gave you particular orders to show his lordship into the library."

"Yes, my lady; but his lordship said he preferred coming here, and followed me in."

The footman retired, and Lord Morlif approached.

"The man is correct. His lordship does prefer intruding upon the ladies; for he was afraid, under your strict duennaship, my dear madam, you would not allow him to see your *protégée*, whom he is so desirous to meet. But oblige me by telling me what all this means,—such grave faces, and such a cool reception." He approached Gertrude as he spoke, and resting his hand upon the leaves of the fern-book before her, looked in her face in a most familiar manner, and in a still more familiar tone of voice said—

"What does my little friend mean by treating me in this way,—not give me her hand? What have I done?" Gertrude shrank from him and trembled violently.

"Lord Morlif!" exclaimed Lady Elizabeth, looking extremely earnest, "I request you will leave my young friend alone. There is a matter between us which has to be discussed, and I shall trouble you to come with me immediately into the next room."

"Pardon me, my dear Lady Elizabeth, I cannot submit to such an arrangement. What you have to say, and what I have to communicate in return, must transpire in Miss Lewis's presence. It really is absurd; what can have happened?" Again he stooped down close to Gertrude, so close that his face nearly touched hers, and repeated, in a playful, coaxing tone—

"Gertrude dear, *you* will perhaps enlighten me."

Gertrude felt as if her tongue were utterly paralyzed. All she could do was to push him away, looking imploringly towards Lady Elizabeth, who immediately drew near her.

"Come," said she, taking hold of her hand, "you had better leave the room, my dear Gertrude."

"If Miss Lewis leaves the room, madam, our interview must be prorogued. I will have a third person present, and that no other than my fair friend here. I am in earnest; I have no intention to be trifled with."

Gertrude sank back into her chair. "Let me remain," said she; "perhaps it is better I should."

While Lord Morlif stood addressing Lady Elizabeth, Gertrude sat motionless, with her eyes fixed upon his face as if they had been mesmerized. She was in his hands, and dreaded his plausible tongue, but was still ignorant and little prepared for what that tongue could do in attempting to injure her in the eyes of her best friend.

"Well, madam, what is it you have to impart of such importance? I am your most obedient, ready, as in the days of my youth, to stand fire."

"First, my lord, I would speak of that letter you wrote last night to Miss Lewis. She gave it into my hands without breaking the seal. I perused it carefully, and could come to no other conclusion than that it was the production of a man totally devoid of honour, uprightness, and good feeling."

"Thank you, madam."

"I had long heard of your intriguing propensities, but little dreamed a revelation of your baseness would come so directly under my own eyes as it has done. Within the last four-and-twenty hours, my lord, I need scarcely say how painfully distressed I am to find what advantage you take of youth and inexperience."

" Youth and inexperience—" repeated Lord Morlif, with a sardonic laugh, and glancing at both his companions. " We are forming quite a scene for the stage. Pray, madam, proceed; let me hear all you have to say against me, and then I shall take my own counsel in my defence."

" I am sorry to say, my lord, your nefarious conduct stands in need of a stronger tongue and a stronger hand than I have, to handle you as you deserve to be handled. I regret Captain Lewis is not here, to protect his child and manifest his resentment. Having persecuted her with attentions, and done all in your power to change her character and destroy her simplicity, your conduct merits severe impeachment; and were it in my power, I would do so unhesitatingly, for the sake of an example to others."

"Allow me, my dear madam, to speak. There is not the slightest occasion for this warmth, or for abusing a poor man in this unreflecting manner. Permit me to state, the word 'persecuting' is quite erroneous. My little friend here never, I assure you, led me to suppose my addresses were ill received. On the contrary, we have always been excellent friends: have we not, Gertrude — most excellent friends?"

Gertrude would have given much to have had command over her feelings at that moment, but the very struggling for power rendered her powerless. She could not articulate a syllable, and yet felt that appearances were going against her."

"She knows we have been excellent friends; and if I have not been *quite* 'en règle,' that is her own fault, as she has given me ample discretion upon every occasion to respond to her bewitching smiles and attractive eyes. Pray, my dear madam, what can a poor man do, when he is waylaid by such attractions as are to be found here, without falling into a snare?"

"Lord Morlif, I beg of you to desist from speaking in this loose way. You have been insulting enough to my sex already. The subject is likely to be serious, and I am in no way inclined to gloss over your infamy. That letter, my lord, is a shield, is it not, for your thickly-woven excuses? Do not attempt to equivocate. You are well aware you have persecuted my young friend, and saying she gave you discretion is a wicked falsehood. I have perfect confidence in Miss Lewis: she has never, I am convinced, given you encouragement, whatever you maintain."

"What! madam, do you think that letter would ever have been written had she not given me encouragement? You little know what your friend's character is; I am aware of what you are not. She has not been nurtured in her early years in a land of intrigue without being tainted by it. Educated by a man of Lewis's description, she has, as might be expected, a knowledge far beyond her years.

I am not to blame, I assure you I am not to blame. Given to intrigue, you tell me I am. Ha! ha! my young friend knows how to meet me half-way, then."

He bit his lips, and turned round and faced Gertrude.

"Not handsome conduct of you, Gertrude, I must say, but cowardly; for the moment you get into a mess with your sighing Lothario and his mother, you fling your weapons at me, in hopes you may make it appear in their eyes you are free from censure. Lady Elizabeth, you will find your young friend out some of these days. Instead of being a prize for your son, as you in your innocence suppose her to be, she is by no means *sans tache*, but has, on the contrary, more *savoir faire* in these matters than you, or even I, a few weeks back would have given her credit for."

"Lord Morlif," cried Lady Elizabeth in an agitated voice, "I will not listen to these falsehoods. You have already sufficiently defamed my young friend, without repeating another insult. I do not come to you for Gertrude Lewis's character; I am better able to read it than yourself. It is outrageous conduct to treat a good girl in this shameful way, to injure her in the eyes of her best friends if possible. A little while ago, you professed a deep regard for her: shame on you, my lord, shame on you!"

"Not so fast, my dear madam. *En résumé*, you don't, then, believe me; you don't believe Miss Lewis gave me encouragement, and that we have been on most intimate terms all the time you were in Denbighshire? You don't believe me, then?"

Lord Morlif folded his arms, while his face looked as if it had been whitewashed, and glanced at Gertrude with one of his sharp under-looks, as he concluded his phrase in a freezing, taunting tone.

"Intentionally,—no, my lord, certainly not."

"Do you hear that, Miss Lewis? When you have such a friend at court as Lady

Elizabeth, you show your wisdom in keeping on neutral ground, and attempting no recrimination. But do not be elated, my little friend; you are not yet out of the wood. Truth will show itself. Miss Lewis, you maintain, madam, never gave me any encouragement. I will prove it to you she did."

As he spoke the concluding sentence, he fixed his eyes upon Lady Elizabeth, who, with an involuntary shudder, exclaimed—

"How sad it is to think, my lord, that you who have grown-up daughters, and a man of your age, should be so vindictive and malicious towards an unprotected, innocent girl, whom, even if she had given you encouragement, and had shown womanly weakness, you ought to have been the last person to malign—the last at whom you should level your shafts, and expose in this shameful, false, and cruel manner! I pity your progeny, my lord; I pity those who have any relation with you. I earnestly hope there are few such characters in the world."

"Most complimentary, my lady," said Lord Morlif, biting his lips, and growing pale and then livid from suppressed anger. "I wish my friend Gwynne had been present, to have made a memorandum of what passed, and have seen that his lady, upon some occasions, can show so much spirit. The only thing to be regretted is, that she should have put herself in this exhausting state of excitement, for a young lady who is less a subject for her commiseration than her censure. Without further delay, I will show clear evidence against the young lady in question. You require strong proofs, Lady Elizabeth, to shake your faith, and you shall have them. Allow me to claim your attention for a few minutes."

He took out of his pocket a manuscript book, and immediately produced some sketches, which he laid separately upon the table.

"When you look at those wild, imaginary subjects, one glance, madam, is quite sufficient to satisfy you whose little fingers have been at work upon them. Perhaps you will acknowledge these were sweet pretty *souvenirs* for one who persecuted her with his attentions. This I look upon as the greatest treasure of all, this miniature. What do you think of that, madam, as a gift from the young lady who wishes to make you believe I persecuted her with attentions? A strange way—a very strange way, indeed, of manifesting her annoyance! My mistake is pardonable, you must own. Whose veracity is to be trusted for the future? Have I at last convinced you, madam?"

With the miniature in her hand, the bewildered lady sank upon the sofa, looking towards Gertrude for an explanation. If Gertrude, after all, had deceived her, how should she ever recover such a blow? Her poor son, too, for him it was ten thousand times worse. Short as the moment was, it was one of intense pain.

Gertrude no sooner saw the expression of grief in Lady Elizabeth's face, than, as if by magic, she rose from her chair, and, with a self-possession which she never before exhibited, and which it seemed impossible she could muster, but equal to the occasion, she approached Lady Elizabeth with a firm step, incited by indignation, and said, in a resolute tone—

"Do not, I implore you, Lady Elizabeth, believe him. He speaks the grossest falsehoods; every word he has uttered is a falsehood. I never gave him those sketches, nor the miniature; indeed I never did. They were once Mrs. Parry's, and I did not know till this moment they were in Lord Morlif's possession. Whether his lordship purloined them, or how he obtained them, it is not for me to explain. They were her property, not mine, given to her by myself. If my father were here, he would make his lordship explain this dishonourable transaction."

"Miss Lewis," replied Lord Morlif, looking her boldly in the face, "is it possible you can utter such an untruth? Do you dare to say Mrs. Parry gave those sketches to me?"

"I do, my lord; or else that you obtained them surreptitiously—one or the other."

"A most deceitful way of getting out of the scrape! Because you know that poor woman cannot give her evidence, you think you are safe in making such a statement."

"And you, my lord, for the same reason, rest secure from an exposition that would shame you, were you capable of feeling shame."

"This is going a little too far. Why can't you have the candour to confess you did give them to me, and that we have been on most intimate terms?" returned his lordship; "sitting side by side, too, times out of number, at the tea-table at Clogwyn, speaking unutterable things, you know, Gertrude, with those eyes. It is too bad!" He stooped his head down, and whispered in her ear. Gertrude drew back indignantly, and he persisted in his attempt.

Lady Elizabeth shrank from them, looking more bewildered and confused than ever. Her face changed colour, and she appeared ready to faint. This seemed to arm Gertrude with recruited energy; she pushed Lord Morlif's head away, and said—

"How dare you, my lord, thus heap insult upon insult?" Turning to Lady Elizabeth, she continued—

"I see you do not believe me. I have no witness to disprove these wicked statements. This moment Lord Morlif stooped and whispered in my ear to confess it — to confess what is false, and he will stand my friend. In the hands of so base a man, Lady Elizabeth, I am powerless. I stand arraigned before you. How can I clear myself? Before my Creator, the Judge of all hearts, I am innocent of these disgraceful, these cruel charges. I call on that great Being to shield me. Never before this hour had Lord Morlif the audacity to call me by my Christian name; never before did he dare to treat me with this familiarity." Gertrude felt her courage rise, if possible, yet higher. " This is a subtle attempt to make me appear guilty in your eyes, Lady Elizabeth ; you cannot credit such a cowardly wretch, such a traducer of a helpless girl. Would my father were here! he would make him devour his own words. You cannot credit such a monster of falsehood, dear Lady Elizabeth."

Here Gertrude seemed exhausted by an effort so contrary to her natural character.

Yarico, who had felt persuaded something was going on wrong, had been wandering about the house. At this moment she caught the sound of her mistress's broken voice, apparently in emotion, and then in distress. Without ceremony she entered the room. Slowly her brawny, athletic frame moved up to her mistress, and she exclaimed, in angry tones—

"What you do to my missus? Nobody shall touch my missus—nobody shall hurt her."

The negress's eyes flashed fire as she stood facing Lord Morlif, as if demanding an explanation. He was in such a position that the light shone full upon his face. Yarico's dark gaze instantly became fixed upon his countenance, and she repeated, in a sneering tone—

"It is you, after all—you fiend, you devil! I not know dat man was de same as dis Lord Morlif. I know now you are dat man who had eyes like nobody else, and a tongue like nobody else. You white devil! what have you been doing to my missus? If you have put your hand upon her, may the fire burn you!—if you have been using your black tongue, may it be dried up to a cinder! My massa shall know dis; and he will make your bones feel it, too, you mean coward! Why was it Yarico was not told before dat Lord Morlif was dat man?—she would have spit in his face before he came to Clogwyn."

Yarico's excitement soared to such a height, it rose almost to a convulsion, in her attempt to restrain herself from seizing him in her powerful grasp, from which his dissipated frame could not have enabled him to escape easily. Suddenly she took her mistress's arm, and almost lifted her off her feet, to get her out of Lord Morlif's presence: and thus she made her perforce leave the room.

What followed between Lady Elizabeth and her visitor was summary, and of a very angry character. Lord Morlif forgot himself in his language; Lady Elizabeth then rang the bell, and ordered the servant to show Lord Morlif the hall-door.

There was a hubbub in the servants' hall soon after the nobleman's departure. Jones said he had a good mind to kick his lordship out, as he showed him the door. He had behaved shamefully, and had made his poor mistress look like a corpse. Margaret was sitting in a dark corner, crying. Williams the butler, an hour later, walked about the dining-room in a state of bewilderment, and gave himself four journeys for one before he had completed his duties there. At last, standing before the fire and rubbing his hands, he said—

"Well, I have seen my master in a good many towering passions, but never in my life witnessed one that would come up to such as I saw to-day. Good gracious! to think of a nobleman putting himself into such fume, and in my lady's presence, too, all on account of this quiet Miss Lewis! He may bless his stars her father was not here, or he would have broken every bone in his mealy, waxy-looking skin; and that would have been just the exact thing he deserved. He has given my poor missus trouble before now—should not I like to have free play at whacking him!"

CHAPTER VI.

A week after the foregoing scene, Lady Elizabeth and Gertrude were taking their lunch in the breakfast-room, when Jones announced Mr. Gilford. Both started: the former rose hurriedly, with the intention of meeting him in the hall, when the gentleman made his appearance.

"An unexpected pleasure! I am glad to see you, Mr. Gilford," were the first words that greeted him. "Where have you left Anarawd? You have brought him with you—say you have?" She looked behind the short, thick figure that stood before her, as if expecting to see her son's beaming face.

Then came the look of disappointment. "He is not here, then, and you have left him abroad! Oh, Mr. Gilford! why did you not bring him back to England? My dear, dear boy!" She burst into tears. Gertrude's face was extremely pale, and Mr. Gilford felt the awkwardness of his position: he, however, attempted to soothe the poor mother's grief by informing her that he had left her son in Heidelberg, looking uncommonly well; and that he was a fine, noble fellow, that England might be proud of. In reply to some of Lady Elizabeth's questions, he entered more into particulars, and delivered Anarawd's messages almost as emphatically as if they had been delivered by the young man himself.

"As happy there, as he would be were he in Oxford?" repeated Lady Elizabeth, with a lugubrious movement of the head. "You are equivocating: he is not happy, but hankering after his home—you know it to be true."

"Well, my dear Lady Elizabeth, if he is not as happy abroad as in his own country, I can assure you that no young fellow ever enjoyed himself more among the Alps than he did. In searching after the picturesque, we lost him entirely for three days; and a terrible fright he put me into!"

"How like him! I envy you, Mr. Gilford, at having been so lately in his company. I shall weary you with questions; but you must bear with me."

Mr. Gilford assured her that he had come expressly for that purpose; that Anarawd would not rest until he had promised to be the bearer of numberless messages; that her son was anxious about her health, and he was afraid he could not give him a satisfactory account, for he never remembered to have seen her looking so delicate as she did at the present time.

"The autumn never suits me; and the separation from my son is a bitter trial."

"You should indeed, my dear madam, endeavour to be reconciled to his absence. You have your young friend here to cheer you."

Mr. Gilford's eye rested with not a little interest upon Gertrude, whom he had not seen before, but of whom he had heard so much. She was completing a small purse, most elaborately worked. He guessed for whom it was intended, and thought what would the poor fellow not have given to be in his place on the present occasion, instead, as he doubtless was, poring over his mathematics in the gloomy apartment in the castle court at Heidelberg.

After rummaging in his pocket, he handed Gertrude a small parcel which Anarawd had commissioned him to give her, and was at once struck with the expression which lighted up her features. He began to think he was not, after all, disappointed in her person. She wanted, perhaps, a little more colour; but there was something remarkably sweet about her, and such grace in her movements!

"Well!" ejaculated Mr. Gilford, again turning to Lady Elizabeth. He never could keep upon one subject long together, without growing fidgety. "What a scandalous neighbourhood this is! I have not been in the country half an hour, when a host of strange reports are poured into my ears. So Lord Morlif has left Bryn-y-Coed in debt, and gone to Paris for the winter? A pretty affair that was of Captain Sands', who is no captain at all, eloping with his lordship's second daughter! I understand it is a positive fact; and a glorious mess they have got into! It turns out that these two stars that have been figuring about all the summer, are the sons of a hairdresser in London, who, in order to keep up appearances, have been draining their old father's pocket; and, with all the drainage, they have left the country in debt. A most desirable connection for his lordship! A strange set you have had in the country this summer!"

"I am thankful they are gone," was the only remark Lady Elizabeth made. She then asked Mr. Gilford what his plans were; that she hoped he would make Bleddyn his head-quarters, and visit his friends at such times as might suit him.

Mr. Gilford expressed his gratitude, and said she was always so kind and considerate, but he was afraid he could only remain a few days; during that time he hoped to succeed in cheering her. He then added that he was anxious to run over the hill, to see his old friend Cad Maurice, that afternoon, before dinner, if possible.

"That can easily be accomplished; only, before you start, indulge me by answering a few more questions. Have you seen Mr. Gwynne?"

"A—hem!" Mr. Gilford, having cleared his throat, paused. He was approaching a tender point, and would willingly have avoided the question. Yes, he had called on Mr. Gwynne, and had dined with him the day before he left London.

"What arrangements, then, has he made for Anarawd?" asked Lady Elizabeth, eagerly.

Again Mr. Gilford looked uneasy, and hesitated before he gave her the information that Mr. Gwynne had decided to keep him at Heidelberg till he got his commission, which he supposed could hardly be later than the spring.

"Oh, Mr. Gilford! am I not, then, to see him at all? Is he to go from his studies to his regiment?"

Mr. Gilford said he would have to go through his examination—perhaps have a week or two's leave.

The colour came and went in Lady Elizabeth's face. She remarked, with some bitterness, "that he might have finished his studies at Oxford, and have come occasionally to see her. To deprive her of the greatest comfort she had, rended the mother's heart, and made her ready to break into open rebellion."

"No, that would be most impolitic, my dear madam. It is better for you both to submit: Mr. Gwynne is more likely to work round by this means, and be reconciled in time to your and your son's wishes. That is the cardinal point. We should look at it in that view."

"Ah!" ejaculated Lady Elizabeth, despairingly, "I know Mr. Gwynne better than you do, Mr. Gilford, though you were so many years under our roof. There will be no amity between father and son as long as they live. I do not look for it."

"You take the gloomy side of the picture; I take the sunny side. There is nothing like being hopeful in getting through this stormy world. Hope is balm to the heart and balm to the brain, the elixir of life! Pray hear me: I have one thing to say in favour of Heidelberg. There, unlike

Oxford, he will have nothing to divert or unsettle him. He will be able to pursue his studies without interruption; and work, you may rest assured, will do him good."

"You are no friend of mine, Mr. Gilford, I perceive. I believe you have been persuading Mr. Gwynne to keep him there. I thought you had more sympathy for a mother—more feeling in you."

"Indeed you wrong me. I assure you, before and since I returned to England, I have done all in my power to prevail upon Mr. Gwynne to consent to his son's return; but I failed: therefore, what can we do but make the best of it? I am strongly opposed to an open rupture, which, you are aware, my dear lady, would be a most serious disadvantage to your son at the present moment. Let him come of age; let him get his commission. These points should be considered. I have weighed the matter well in my mind, and have spoken seriously to your son, for whom I must ever feel a deep and lasting interest. Recollect, there is the *pro* and the *con.* in all these affairs, and hasty actions and hasty judgments are not advisable."

" You have not a son, Mr. Gilford—you have not a son. You do not know what it is to be a paernt. How shall I ever exist through the winter without his dear face to cheer me ?"

" Look forward to the spring."

" I may not live to the spring. I feel my health giving way. I may never see my boy again !"

She sat back in her chair, and once more burst into tears.

Mr. Gilford walked towards the window, took out his handkerchief and coughed.

Gertrude, thinking Lady Elizabeth might prefer being alone for a time, and anxious also to examine the parcel which Anarawd had sent her, had stolen out of the room a few minutes before.

The moment she reached the hall, she took a cloak off the stand, and wrapping it about her, hurried away into the garden.

Late as it was in the year, the day was moist and genial: the sun was shining brightly, and the robins were chirping merrily upon the boughs and hopping upon the walk before her. So mild was the season, that, in some of the sheltered nooks, spring flowers and bright green shoots from the parent stock were to be seen struggling into existence.

Taking her eyes off for an instant from the treasured packet which had been monopolizing every thought from the time she had left the house, she looked around upon the landscape. It was a fair scene. Though it was winter, and the trees were generally stripped of their leaves, the hills and the rocks had undergone no change. They looked the same unchangeable things, those eternal hills, just the same as on a smiling summer's day; their colouring was even richer, perhaps, arising from the contrast of the faded fern and discoloured foliage.

Her heart was overcome at the moment, and she could not help exclaiming—

"Oh, how calm, how beautiful, how peaceful is everything around! Ought I not to be calm and peaceful, too, with those tokens of his unshaken affection? Possessing such affection, what have I to fear? There should be no misgivings in my heart. Papa will see his worth."

The moment she caught sight of Mr. Gilford crossing the fields, she returned to the house with a more happy expression on her face than had been seen before since the young heir's absence. Hurrying through the veranda, she stopped before the breakfast-room window, and peeped in to look for Lady Elizabeth.

"Do come out for a walk: the air is delicious. It will do you good," said Gertrude, who had succeeded in attracting her attention.

Lady Elizabeth thought a walk would do her more good than a drive—she would counter-order the carriage, and join her in a few minutes.

In a quarter of an hour they were wandering at a distance from the house. They scarcely noticed how wet the walks were, under the bright blue canopy, and soft, balmy atmosphere. Lady Elizabeth was momentarily cheered by Anarawd's account of his amusing adventures, which Gertrude read to her as they went along.

" We are strolling too far from home — let us now return," said Lady Elizabeth: " the least exertion fatigues me."

Gertrude looked distressed, as her eyes rested upon Lady Elizabeth's features; they bore an expression she had never noticed before, and her face was unusually pale.

" You had better rest a little upon this seat," suggested Gertrude, putting down a shawl : " that will keep the damp away."

" Thank you, my little friend. There is such a sickness come upon my heart! Oh, Gertrude! no language can find utterance to express my disappointment at Mr. Gilford's returning to England without my dear Anarawd. To leave him there, in that wretched country, to pass his winter alone, without a friend or companion near! Would he were here!"

Gertrude was silent; she could not offer consolation, though her heart was swelling with sympathy.

From that day a visible change had come over Lady Elizabeth; nothing seemed to cheer or revive her. She caught a violent cold from remaining out so late that evening; it settled upon her chest. Mr. Gilford had come and gone, and had failed in his attempts to reconcile her to her separation from her son. He had released her from suspense, it was true; but it was only to hear of a cruel, continued separation.

Regrets are useless, every one says, in the way of false comfort. Sermons and homilies, tracts and cottage lectures, all preach the same. It is easy to say, "Never murmur, never regret; it brings no comfort, no good; it is wrong:" and yet how often we do murmur and we do regret! It is a part of our nature. Saint and sinner are not exempt; all murmur, and all go murmuring onwards to the same inevitable bourn. Such is human frailty!

Bleddyn was at this period too full of murmurings and regrets. There was not an individual in the kitchen, stable, or garden department, that was not repining at the absence of the young master, and lamenting over the ill health of their mistress. One would have gone a year without his wages just to have seen the heir amongst them again; another said he would have gone three successive days over the preserves without a mouthful of victuals between his teeth, just to hear his whistle, and see the dogs jumping about him; a third, that he would willingly groom his horse down for him ten times in a day, and sit up for him every night when he chose to go to Clogwyn, if he could only have him there again; he did not care about the trouble, that was nothing. As long as the son of Bleddyn was at home, it was all they wanted. In the sick chamber it was the same, and in the heart of his young betrothed; all wanted him home. Never did Bleddyn look so cheerless: the weather, too, had become damp and stormy, and for a whole week the rain never ceased to pour down in torrents.

CHAPTER VII.

"You must not, my dear Gertrude, be sitting in this warm room all day. The clouds have disappeared from those hills, and the sun is coming out; I think it does not rain now. Go for a brisk walk before dinner."

"Not raining! really not raining, I declare; you won't like my leaving you."

"Yes, for your own sake I wish it. You have read to me long enough, my dear; the air will refresh you, and do you good."

Gertrude rose, and in her own gentle way moved the pillows about the invalid's head as she sat in the chair, and then kissed her.

"What should I do without you, my Gertrude? We seem, since all the late stormy affairs, to be more drawn to each other than ever. There now, I am quite comfortable; no one places a pillow like my dear little friend: bless you! One more kiss, and then go—go while it is fine— the weather is fitful."

"I think my walk shall be to the torrent: after all the rain, I am sure it will be in a troubled state, just in perfection. Look out of the window, and you will see me— farewell."

Thoroughly clad for storm and rain, Gertrude left the warm and comfortable house, and hurried across the fields with Anarawd's retrievers, thinking a walk would do them as much good as herself. The air invigorated her, and she never stopped till she reached the rustic bridge which had been thrown across a wild part of the torrent, almost concealed amongst the woods.

It had ever been a favourite spot. She had often been before upon those planks where she was now standing, with one hand clinging to the railing, and looking down into the angry waters. Slippery as it was, she kept her footing, and never once took her eyes off the great body of water tumbling into foam under her feet, and roaring and bellowing over its rocky bed, almost deafening her. To all appearances, she was under a charm, as she continued watching the surge plunging and breaking over the large stones below. It was not really thus: she could see other objects, and was thinking of very different things. Lady Elizabeth's emaciated frame was now uppermost in her thoughts. What an unkind, unfeeling husband was Mr. Gwynne! Never once had he been down to see his amiable wife, although he knew her state of health. He still persisted in keeping her son from coming home. It was cruelty—more than cruelty, if possible. She could not understand how any heart that beat could prompt its owner to conduct so unfeeling. Poor Anarawd! if he lost his mother, he would never recover her loss—never forgive himself that he had kept abroad, when she was so anxious to have him home. How sad it was to see her fading away, and to feel that nothing could be done to check the inroad of disease, while she could not have even the few and short-lived earthly comforts she wanted! Lady Elizabeth had been united to a being who had in the first instance deceived, and then cruelly neglected her; proving himself in every way unworthy of her virtues. Wretched must be the married state, when there is no sympathy of taste and no congeniality of principles. Such a position in life is, indeed, the least to be envied, the saddest of social exhibitions.

Gertrude had been standing some time, with a succession of similar thoughts to these, when she felt some one catch hold of her by the mantle, and heard a voice roar in her ears, above the roaring of the torrent.

"Take care; it is wet and slippery; take care, or you will tumble. It is raining fast, and you will catch cold." A little old woman stood before her; again she pulled Gertrude by the mantle, and pointed to her cottage.

It was impossible, with the torrent thundering in her ears, to carry on a dialogue. The alternative was to follow the woman submissively, which she did.

"I hope you not too proud to come into my cottage?" said the peasant, as she ascended the broken steps and showed her visitor the way.

Gertrude smiled, and replied she was much obliged to her for offering her a shelter. The little old woman bustled about, and soon placed a seat near the chimney-corner for her guest, while she remained standing before the fire with her knitting.

"You come from Bleddyn, I think—yes?"

"Yes," replied Gertrude.

"I hope missus is better?"

"Not much."

"Oh dear! I sorry in my heart. And the husband of Bleddyn not come back—no?"

"No; Mr. Gwynne is in London."

"Pity, pity! and the son of Bleddyn not come home! Poor missus! she break her heart about it—yes?"

"She would be glad indeed to see him."

"Yes, I am sure, the son of Bleddyn is such a good young man. He got such a kind way with the mother! I see no young gentleman like him; no, indeed. When he was a little boy he often come to my cottage, and never passes my house now without calling out 'Nelly.' He is very funny, you know. He laugh and tell like this: 'Well, Nelly, do you still keep the kettle boiling, and the cupboard full of oat-cake and butter?' Then he look very sly, and I see him drop a bit of money on the step, and take up his fishing-rod and go quite quick over the bridge, and afterwards call out—'That's for good luck, Nelly, till we meet again.' Indeed, he is very kind, and a fine young gentleman, too. I vex not about the money, but because I no see his face this long while. Where is he now?"

"In Germany."

"That is very far off; I hear the people talk about that country."

"You have to cross the seas to go to it."

"Poor missus! she break her heart!—I am sure she break her heart!"

Taking the opportunity of the first pause, the woman went to her cupboard, and brought out a pile of oat-cakes, and a basin of butter.

"Let me give you some oat-cake. I make the oat-cake this morning. It is quite fresh."

"Not any, thank you."

"No—you too proud?"

"No, I am not too proud; but I am

going to dine when I get home, and I have had my luncheon."

" Oh, never mind, take a little. Perhaps you no like oat-cake? I have rye-bread baked in a pan. Will you have some of that? It is very good."

Gertrude was amused, and assured her she could not take anything. But the woman was not satisfied, being bent upon giving her guest something. With that intention, she left the apartment, and disappeared behind a boarded partition.

While she was away, Gertrude had ample time to look around. The dwelling could boast of but little comfort. From a small window, sunk deep in the unplastered wall, with an old stocking filling up the broken pane, her eyes wandered to a corner where a heap of turf was piled up; and close in its vicinity stood a barrel, two peat-baskets, a basket of potatoes, and a spade. On the opposite side was a large spinning-wheel, on the top of which sat a grave-looking cat, that had evidently perched herself there to get out of the way of her kitten's gambols. Before the window—if it may be called a window—stood a wooden table, roughly put together, and much discoloured by time and usage. Then there was the dresser. Everything gave way to that important piece of furniture, always the centre of attraction in a Welsh cottage. The household treasures were there displayed, arranged upon it in the most precise order. As a whole, it looked rather out of keeping with the rest of the rickety and poverty-stricken furniture. There was no fireplace upon the hearth, but a few large stones served for a grate. The fire burned and crackled cheerfully beneath a large black pot suspended over it, in a state of ebullition. Propped up by an iron frame, some oat-cakes were drying and crisping at a little distance, and looked in character with the place. Brooms appeared scarce; the floor, if it were not of mud, bore a strong resemblance to it, and did not add much to the appearance of comfort in the living-room. The poverty here so apparent did not affect Nelly's spirits. She had a happy-looking face, and there was the same willing tendency about her to say a kind word and make others comfortable which had ever marked her character. It is true, she had her own idea of comfort and happiness, and they were really comfort and happiness to her.

Gertrude was not inclined to be critical. When Nelly re-appeared, she held in one hand the skin of an American bird, and in the other a small glass of whisky.

"Now, you must take this from me as a present," said she, holding up the gay stuffed bird; "and you must drink this to keep out the wet and cold. It will do you good; yes, I am sure."

Gertrude could not help laughing. The idea of her sipping whisky in that odd-looking chimney-corner, with the two great dogs on one side of her, and the singular little old woman on the other—it was quite a picture.

Again she laughed: "Really, Nelly, I am sorry not to oblige you; but I can't take it. I do not like whisky."

"Not like whisky? Oh, pity! My son bring this from Ireland; and it is so good! He tell me it is prime stuff. The gentlemen in this country, he is sure, would be glad enough to have it in their cellars."

"It may be good, Nelly; but I do not like spirits."

Nelly cast up her eyes in amazement. "What a strange thing not to like such nice warming stuff! A little glass like that of a night keep away the cold, and make me so comfortable! But I do not often get it; only when my son come from sea."

"I must go now," said Gertrude, rising and peeping out of the deep-set window. "Do you think it rains still?"

The old woman said, it was raining

worse than ever; she could not go; but when she did, she must take care of the wet planks, lest she should slip into the torrent. To her it was always the same, whether she went over it by night or day, dry or wet weather; but then she was used to it.

Gertrude remarked that she thought she could do the same; upon which assertion, the woman looked incredulous, and persisted that all young ladies grew giddy in the head; that she had often been obliged to conduct strangers across the bridge, it was so dangerous.

"You are a sort of guide, then, to the bridge, and get something for your trouble, I hope?"

"Yes," replied Nelly, nodding her head and smiling archly; but I have nobody to thank but the son of Bleddyn; he has given me many a loaf, and not know of it."

"What do you mean?"

Nelly eyed her companion with an expression of surprise: did she not know what all the country knew, that the son of Bleddyn, when a little boy, had saved his pocket-money to build the bridge, because the poor about there wanted to go sharp to the village, and found it most inconvenient?

No, she had not heard it.

"He was a prettier little boy, much prettier than he is now he is older," continued Nelly abstractedly. "He looks now more serious in the face. I think, indeed, the father brings trouble on him; Mr. Gwynne is not a nice man." In a more confidential manner, Nelly dropped her voice, and said, "Don't you tell, but I hear the people in the country say, Mr. Gwynne is not kind to his son, and now is more angry than ever with him, because he wants to marry Miss Lewis, that proud young lady that everybody talks about. She is so beautiful, and so grand; have you ever seen her?"

"Yes," replied Gertrude, not sorry that

the cottage was dark, and that the woman could not see her face.

"And is she very beautiful?"

"Some people may think so."

"I hear she has a very clean-looking skin, and blue eyes and fair hair. Is that true? I should like to see her."

Gertrude nodded her head; she did not disrelish a harmless joke, and was enjoying it under her cloak in the dark corner, but had difficulty in controlling her mirth.

Nelly went on in her own peculiar strain —"I am sorry she is proud. They tell in the chapels that to be proud is very wicked. I not like the son of Bleddyn's wife to be proud — pity, pity he give his heart to her. I vex — indeed I vex!"

"If the son of Bleddyn does marry her, I suppose his wedding-day will be a day of mourning instead of one of rejoicing among you tenants?"

"Yes, indeed, I think so. Don't you see, we want a good wife for the son of Bleddyn."

" What would you call a good wife ?"

" Why, some one like missus, that take notice of us poor people; and not a lady, that would be thinking of her pretty face and fine clothes, and making a great company in the house every day."

" You are right, Nelly; I am afraid there is little hope of such a young lady as you describe. You must put on mourning when the day comes; I will come and condole with you."

" Perhaps, after all, the people tell stories in the country. I wish in my heart I could see her face; I always know by the face if there is anything good in a stranger. Indeed, I wish I could see her; I only wish that."

" She was walking near the bridge, the other day, in an old cloak and hat: it is a pity you did not see her then."

" No, that's not possible; Miss Lewis is always driving and riding about the country. She is too grand—she would never wear an old cloak, and walk out in bad weather."

"I think it was she; I shall bring her to see you some day, Nelly," said Gertrude, much diverted.

"No, no," cried the little old woman in a state of great agitation, "she would be too proud to come into this dirty little place. She would make quite a fright come upon me."

"Why should she alarm you? I will bring her, Nelly. It is a pity you should not have your wish gratified. You shall see her."

"No, indeed, you must not bring her here; my heart would jump into my mouth, I should be so frightened."

In her excitement, she threw some gorse upon the fire, and the cottage in a moment was in a blaze of light.

Now, thought Gertrude, this is not *mal à propos*. Dropping her cloak, and removing her hat and veil, she suddenly placed herself before the woman, with her fair hair falling over her shoulders, and, with one of her hearty laughs, saying—

"You have your wish, Nelly; you see the proud Miss Lewis now; you have an opportunity of judging if you think she will make the son of Bleddyn a good wife."

The little old woman was struck dumb. With her mouth open, and her eyes fixed, she drew back astounded and pale.

"Don't be frightened, Nelly; you see I am not too proud to come into your cottage, nor too grand to run over here on a wet day in an old cloak, which has served me for an admirable disguise."

Quite overcome, the poor woman sank down upon a three-legged stool, and began to shed tears, and rock herself to and fro, exclaiming—

"Indeed, indeed, young lady, I am sorry for what I have said. O that foolish tongue of mine! What shall I do? you will not forgive me!"

"Yes, I would, if there were any forgiveness required. I am glad you said what you did; it is always well to know what is thought of us in the neighbourhood where we reside. Pray don't distress yourself, then, Nell. Shake hands, and let us be friends, in spite of what the people say."

Gertrude smiled again and again at the startled face of the poor woman, and patted her on the arm; but, with all her encouragement, Nelly could not forgive herself, crying and laughing alternately. Gertrude now felt it was high time to quit the cottage.

"I must go," said she, "if it is raining or not, for it is getting dark; and you will help me on with my cloak, and be a lady's maid for once in your life to the proud Miss Lewis. It will be something for you to think of when I am gone. And here is this, besides, to occupy your mind. Since the son of Bleddyn is too far off to leave a remembrance in your cottage for good luck, let me execute the trust in his behalf. Accept a present from the daughter of Clogwyn." As she spoke, she laid half a sovereign upon the table.

The little old woman eyed the coin in

bewilderment, and tears started to her eyes. "No, no, she could not have the heart to take it, when she had treated her so unkindly, and had called her proud."

"Unkindly? No, Nelly; rather you have done me a service. Take the money, or I shall think you do not wish to be friends."

"No, indeed, young lady, no tell that. I wish to be friends, and am obliged to you a hundred times." While she spoke, she pressed the hem of Gertrude's cloak to her lips. This was Nelly's primitive manner of expressing her gratitude.

As Gertrude groped her way to the door, the old woman followed, repeating—"Stop, stop; let me help you over the bridge—you will fall, it is slippery." But Gertrude was quickly beyond hearing; like a deer, she had sprung over the wet planks, and soon disappeared among the trees.

As she continued on her way to Bleddyn, she thought over the occurrence in the cottage. The poor little woman's look of dismay when she made herself known; her admiration and solicitude for her young master; her interest and commiseration for her mistress; her hospitality, good-nature, and remarkable primitiveness, — were all too striking not to leave their impression upon the mind of Gertrude. She thought it singular that Anarawd had not mentioned the little woman nor the bridge to her, and that Lady Elizabeth had also been silent upon the subject. It was by such simple incidents that the nobleness of Anarawd's character was constantly revealed, enhancing the dignity of his nature. When she looked to the period when first she had become acquainted with him, she blushed at the recollections of her childlike failings. To him she owed much of the elevation of her mind; for love is a great teacher of what is excellent or virtuous when the flame is pure. She had been unconscious of her lover's influence; he had given her new tastes, and led her to appreciate studies which had once been distasteful. Influence, either for good or for evil, takes varied forms, and has no limit. Our intercourse with the noble spirits of the past, through the medium of their never-dying productions, control and spur us on to higher aims. Still, the influence of the past is not so attractive nor so powerful as that emanating from those we love, when in direct communication, and affection's bright rays kindle and stimulate the heart, and create a desire to imitate those cherished objects we so much admire and revere.

The wind still roaring among the leafless branches above her head, and the rain pattering ceaselessly, Gertrude drew a mental comparison between her father and Anarawd Gwynne. She admired in the latter what she had missed in her father: with Anarawd there was no concealment—bold truth dwelt upon his lips; with her father there was that reticence which she could not comprehend, and which made her apprehensive for the future; she felt there was a secret yet to be unfolded, but knew not of what nature that secret might be, or what might follow upon its development. With Anarawd all was lucid and transparent as day. She had misgivings: she might not make him as good a wife as he deserved; he was worthy of a better; still she felt she could not be happy without him. Embarrassing thoughts, as usual, came uppermost, as to how her father would be reconciled to parting from her. To him she was everything the world possessed! She almost wished he did not love her with that adoration. It was a stolen wish, really a foreign one to her affectionate heart—one of those which, like deep shadows of the clouds on the earth's surface, pass rapidly along and dim the sunshine. Her cheeks deepened their colour as the thought flashed across her mind with lightning speed; and as she entered the house, she felt them burning.

CHAPTER VIII.

The air was chill, the heavens lurid; the snow fell fast, and drifted against the hedges; the country looking a wide waste, hoary with age. Nature seemed in the last stage of senility. The birds near a small plantation of hollies were searching for the scarlet berries to appease their hunger; for the ground was buried under the snow, and concealed their winter store of food. The bells were ringing for the afternoon service. Groups of peasants, in their Sunday attire, were threading their way in files over the snowy carpet to church and chapel—their gay umbrellas before their faces, supported with difficulty to repel the drifting element. Christmas had arrived in the midst of the melancholy aspect of Nature. It was not the good jovial Christmas of olden times. At the great house among the trees, responsive and sympathetic melancholy seemed to reign, and expand over the whole vicinity. Not a cheerful face, not a joyful sound was seen or heard within the walls of the old mansion. There every step bespoke a secret something pressing, not only upon the spirit, but upon inanimate things. Feasting was going on in the servants' hall, it was true; but the spirit of joy was not there. Never were plum-pudding and roast beef less appreciated by domestics. They partook of the dishes before them in comparative silence. Not one merry voice came upon the ear, not one joyous laugh was seen upon any countenance. It was well for things to be in unison: sadly would it have jarred upon Gertrude's ear, as she sat in the breakfast-room in a frame of mind harmonizing with the general gloom, and eagerly listening for the roll of the wheels and the sound of the door-bell; for it was at such a moment that Anarawd Gwynne was expected to arrive.

Lady Elizabeth's health had become more impaired. There were no hopes of her recovery. The household lived in expectation of being bereaved of one who had peculiarly endeared herself to them and to the poor around. At the eleventh hour, Mr. Gwynne had consented to his son's return. He himself had been down for a few days, but had gone back again to London. He made everybody at home believe he was overwhelmed with his Parliamentary duties, so that he had not an hour to spare. What his Parliamentary duties were, no one could discover; nothing was done by him for the county he represented, neither for the rich nor for the poor. Still, Mr. Gwynne endeavoured to persuade the people he was working himself into a shadow for his esteemed and valued constituents;

such is the slang of do-nothing Parliamentary men. He was, forsooth, invisible because he was buried among Parliamentary papers and official documents. He succeeded in making some credulous persons believe he was writing upon the corn-laws, pondering over a clever project for local improvements and the legislative expenses for such an undertaking. Nothing of the sort was ever forthcoming. A report, too, began to be circulated, that it was all a mistake; he was not always in London ensconced amongst his papers; Mr. Gwynne, or some one extremely like him, was frequently seen moving about in Paris, not among the more respectable of the *haut-ton*, and that he made himself singular by his attentions to Miss Morlif. When Mr. Gwynne was invisible from his duties in the Metropolis, he was therefore known to be in Paris, indulging in the gaieties of that attractive city, and enjoying the society of the Morlifs, his most esteemed friends.

Such was the unhappy state of affairs regarding the head of the family, at the time when Gertrude, having stolen out of the chamber while Lady Elizabeth was asleep, repaired to the breakfast-room, and was sitting before the fire watching with impatience for her lover's return. Her heart beat with varied emotions. There was the weight of her own grief—the sympathy for Anarawd, who was about to hear distressing news, and must prepare himself for a most severe trial in the loss of an excellent and attached mother. Then there was joy—it seemed strange to have joy creeping in with so much sorrow—at the thought how soon she would be clasped in Anarawd's arms—would see his face, his dear face, and again hear the voice she loved. Absence had but strengthened her affections.

The evening appeared to close in earlier than usual: grotesque shadows were upon the walls and ceiling, while the stillness of the room became almost unbearable. Gertrude had listened until she was weary. No sound of approaching wheels was heard. Why did he not come? The evening darkened more and more, still he did not appear. The fire was nearly out, yet she did not stir to ring the bell. If he would only come, what a relief it would be!

At length the door-bell did ring, without being preceded by the rattling of the carriage. Gertrude started up. Could it be he? Hurrying into the hall, she received the welcome news that it was the young master. The snow was deep, and had deadened the sound of the wheels: the carriage was coming round.

When the door was thrown open, a blast of biting wind came rushing in, and blew out some of the lights; but Gertrude was in a state of too great trepidation to feel the cold air, or think of anything but the one object on which her thoughts were concentrated. There was a slight delay; the servants had gathered round the carriage-door to welcome their young master. Gertrude could scarcely curb her impatience. At last her eager ear caught the sound of his voice; she felt his arm encircled her, and she recollected no more. They came into Anarawd's study, and soon they were seated side by side, his eye resting upon her, pausing and dreading to ask questions, yet wishing to know all he could be told.

On Gertrude breaking to him the precarious state of his mother's health, and mentioning how she had been yearning to see him, Anarawd got up and walked about the room, his eyes dimmed with tears, and his heart too full to speak. After a brief silence, he expressed much impatience to see his mother. Could he go to her then?

Gertrude held his hand. "Prepare yourself, my dearest Anarawd, to see a great change—I am sorry to tell it to you—she is so wasted."

Anarawd flinched under her words, and clasped his hand to his head. " Oh, Gertrude, this is a bitter trial! Is there no hope?"

She had no consolation to offer him. Stifling his anguish, a long, painful silence followed, which was at length broken by Morgan appearing at the door. Lady Elizabeth was anxious to see her young master.

"I will go first," said Gertrude; "you can follow in a few minutes."

His head was bent downwards: a painful sensation had come upon him, and his countenance was sad indeed as he took the light and mounted the staircase. Never had he returned before without feeling a light heart; never had he before missed his mother's warm greeting the first upon his arrival. Scarcely had he reached the threshold of her chamber-door, when her feeble voice broke upon his ear. In a moment he was locked in her arms.

The scene which followed was painfully affecting—too painful for description. The anguish of the son, when his eye encountered his mother's wasted form, excited the pity of all who witnessed it. Gertrude became unnerved and bereft of power. She seemed to feel that a great calamity was suspended over her, that this grief was unlike any grief she had felt before.

The tea-things were upon the table an hour or two afterwards in Anarawd's study, and several dishes of cold meat were arranged, with all the necessary concomitants essential to an Englishman's notion of refreshment in comfort. Everything ought to have been strikingly inviting to a traveller just arrived from comfortless Germany; but Anarawd was too much weighed down with sorrow to regard anything beyond the calamity impending in the state of his mother. In deep sorrow he watched Gertrude pouring out tea. He could partake of nothing else, and evidently of that only because Gertrude sat by his side, and used every possible argument to persuade him to take it.

"I am deeply thankful, my darling Gertrude, to have you with me, and that you have been permitted to be near my mother. What should I have done without you at a moment like the present?"

His lips faltered; Gertrude's hand was clasped in his: she pressed her lips upon his cheek, and whispered him a few words of comfort. Those words only had the effect of bringing fresh tears to his eyes— he was again overcome.

"Leave me, Gertrude, leave me for a time," said he, in a thick voice; "my grief overpowers my reason. Must I part with her for ever?—that being to whom I owe everything in this world! How can I limit my sorrow for such a mother?"

Again he entreated his betrothed to leave him. Gertrude pleaded it was hard he should force her to leave him at such a moment; their hearts were one, their sorrows mutual.

Her look, without the accompanying words, would have been enough; she remained.

The following morning broke on the freezing landscape with a cloudless sky. The white beneath and the azure over all presented a scene of great but chilling beauty. The bright sun of the early morning cast a rosy hue upon the snow-clad hills; the boughs bent beneath their glittering honours, feathered with brilliants; and the birds, half famished, fluttered against the window-panes: earth resembled a desert—a wide waste before the eye of man, for even the beauty of the wintery elements seemed monitory of death.

Gertrude was standing before the window in the invalid's room in deep meditation. Anarawd was sitting by his mother's bedside. She appeared more placid and collected than she had been for many hours, conversing little; but her eyes never wandered from her son's face, and spoke what was going on within. At times there was an anxious expression in her face, but more frequently one of unmingled affection. Her thin, wasted fingers were clasped by those of her son. It seemed as if she would fain retain him, scarcely permitting him to leave her for a single moment.

"I thought you were going," she murmured, as Anarawd changed his position. "The light of this world, I feel, will quickly darken before my eyes; I shall soon behold you no more: therefore, keep near me, my dear boy. Where is Gertrude, my affectionate nurse? She has had much to try her during your absence. Anarawd, my dear, you will never forsake her! Be faithful to her, for she is deserving of your affection."

"My dear mother!—"

"You will not neglect her, nor treat her in any way unkindly, will you?"

"Why doubt it—why question it, my dear mother. She will be all left to me in the world when you are gone. You know how deeply we are attached."

"Yes, yes, only be faithful to her. Where is she?"

Gertrude approached and stood near Anarawd's chair.

"There now, I like to see you together: live and love each other through life."

"Do not doubt it, dearest mother," was once more repeated.

"No, perhaps not; but you are young, and will soon be again tossed about the world. You will be surrounded by evil; and the influence of evil example is great. Do not forsake my poor little Gertrude; do not break her heart—the tender heart she has given you."

Anarawd's earnest eyes rested upon his mother's face; he implored her not to foster any such ideas, that it was impossible he could treat ill one whom he loved so deeply.

Lady Elizabeth closed her eyes, and sank back upon her pillows, exhausted, and muttering to herself; Anarawd bent his head. "Be faithful, be faithful to her."

Young Gwynne, not easy in his mind, got up and stood upon the hearth, looking into the fire, startled and pained at what his mother had said. Gertrude followed him, and put her hand gently into his.

"Do not let her words distress you: she is wandering a little, that is all!"

"I would rather the words had been unsaid. It grieves me, Gertrude, that even the thought should have crossed her mind. I wish she had not said it."

"She is thinking of her own unhappy married life; it perhaps recurs more vividly to her just at the present moment. Do not let it trouble you. How often she has spoken to me of your stability of character! and I know she reposes implicit confidence in you. I have never doubted it, nor ever shall doubt it. Do not, my dearest Anarawd, give the words another thought."

There was something indefinable in Gertrude's manner that found its way to his heart swifter than her words. Never, when his spirit was ruffled, did she fail to soothe him. It was a charm she possessed, a power of restoring him to himself.

Lady Elizabeth began again to ask for her son. A change seemed to come over her; she grew more restless, and her lips became parched. The excitement on her son's arrival, the day before, was evidently telling upon her debilitated frame.

"You appear uncomfortable: shall I move your pillows?"

"No, my dear boy; I only feel the hour is approaching when we must part. It ought not to be so, yet it is a hard struggle. Could I have seen you and Gertrude happily united before I left the world, my heart would have been lighter. Do not be guided by the world; it is a dangerous counsellor. God keep you, my children, from its snares! The pilgrimage of the longest-lived here is soon over. Be provident of the hours allotted to you: they are precious, and an account of them must be rendered."

A long pause followed; then she started as if from a dream.

"Is your father coming to-day?"

"No."

"Then I shall not see him. Tell him he has my forgiveness for the wrongs he has done me from the day we were bound together in marriage. He has my prayers. God Almighty keep him from further evil, and forgive him for the past! You must not grieve for me; I am about to be removed from a scene of sin and sorrow: you must be calm. The finger of God is here, as it is everywhere. Be resigned to His will:—no upbraiding, no murmurings at His dispensations. I am going to where the weary find repose, where we shall meet again. I am weary for want of it. Let me, then, precede you, and do not weep for me."

She now began to draw her breath heavily, and to be more restless. Anarawd supported her in his arms.

"Mistress seems not so well to-day,"

whispered Morgan, who had stolen into the room. " I see a great change. The doctor is here: shall he come up ?"

" No," said Gertrude, " not now; ask him to step into the dining-room. I will come to him presently."

All was again still: Lady Elizabeth's quick breathing grew less distinct. Anarawd was stifling his grief, and some time passed in painful silence.

" Gertrude, she is going !" cried Anarawd, in a thick tone of voice. " She will never speak more to us. Oh, my mother ! my mother !"

His accents seemed to catch her attention and recall her for a moment to herself. She struggled in his arms.

" Where are you, my dear children ?" she exclaimed, looking round.

" Here, mother." And both placing their hands in hers, she clasped them together with a faint smile, and continued—

" I don't like leaving you in this gloomy

world. My sight grows dim; I feel damp and chill—there is a blight coming over everything around me. May it not touch you, my children! Come closer. Oh, could we but go together into the land of rest, and glorify God with united voices for ever! But I must go alone; it is so ordained." Her voice died into a whisper. "Alone! alone!" she repeated, fainter and fainter. She then drew her breath more laboriously, heaved a tremulous gentle sigh, and passed to where sighs and sufferings cease for ever.

CHAPTER IX.

"Massa Gwynne is in the library," said the negress, suddenly appearing before her mistress with a lugubrious countenance. "He no look de same man; so thin, so pale, so broken in de spirit. It make Yarico's heart sick to look at him."

With misgivings, Gertrude crossed the hall and softly opened the library door. Anarawd was sitting with his head upon his hands. He made no attempt to greet her. She took her seat by his side, remaining silent. She knew at that moment nothing she said would reach his sorrow-stricken heart. The pressure of her hand locked in his was a sufficient demonstration of her sympathy. It was still a comfort to be together—the only comfort the world could offer.

That morning Anarawd had followed the remains of his lamented mother to her grave, not as he would have desired, solemnly and silently, but under the customary idle pomp and artificial demonstration of ostensible respect for the dead. The country gentlemen and the tenantry had been invited to a sumptuous breakfast, to regale at the portals of death. This delayed the funeral. The intervening moments lay heavy upon the spirits of the mourning son.

According to the undertaker's pompous arrangements, they followed the hearse in great state to the little church under the hill near the town of Angharad.

That evening, in the servants' hall, the butler declared, with a long face, he was thankful he had got his master to bed before Master Anarawd returned from Clogwyn.

"What! Williams, is master screwed again?" asked the groom, with a broad grin. "I say, the old cock had better mind what he is about, or, as sure as a gun, he won't stand long upon his pins."

The butler shuffled his hands into his pocket, saying, as he seated himself at the table, in a decided tone—

"No, that he won't; he takes more drink than ever. He was mad, quite mad, to-night. I never saw such a pair of eyes, moving round and round, before; no, never. It is something very bad; only to think of poor missus just put into the churchyard, and master in that drunken state, worse than a beast!"

"I don't care if I go to-morrow, now missus is gone," said the old gardener, rising and moving to the fireplace with tears in his eyes.

" Nor I either, nor I either," echoed several voices.

" Well," said Williams, " as long as there's a chance of seeing my young master three weeks in the year, I will keep to my old quarters. That poor young gentleman, if he were my own son, I don't think I could care much more for him."

" Yes, surely, we must all feel for him, that we know. But, Williams, master will marry again; and our young master will never show his face at Bleddyn, nor in town," replied the groom, looking disconsolate.

" Yes, Mills, you are right; master will marry again, and I know to whom," interrupted Jones.

" What! to that young lady who was here in the summer, I suppose you mean?"

" Ay, that's the young lady; she that was always rolling her eyes about, and looking so sweet upon master, whenever missus was out of the room. I saw, and know a great deal, only I don't choose to tell. I know it will be so. If master were drowned to-morrow, I should not care."

"Jones, you don't mean Miss Morlif? I hope to goodness master won't marry her," said Williams, with great gravity.

"Yes, I do; and it will be a match, you will see, before six weeks are over. That's my opinion."

"Shame, shame! don't make master worse than he is."

"It would be difficult to do that," replied the footman, curling up his lips contemptuously.

"I agree with you, Jones," rejoined Morgan; "his heart is as black as his hat. He killed my mistress by his cruel conduct, and has almost broken our young master's heart."

"He will meet his punishment some day, without our praying for it. That's a comfort."

"I hope he may. I will soon get out of this house. Master told me last night he wished me to stay! Do you think I would remain here, and be a lady's-maid to that sharp-eyed, hook-nosed lady? No, if I were offered two hundred a-year. I would rather be a poor girl in a baker's shop, or scrub the floors, or work in the fields at digging up potatoes—that I would!"

"I admire your spirit, Margaret, and think you are right. I should pity any one who was to be her maid. She has a precious temper; you can see it in her mouth. If master marries her, he will find his match. She will lead him the life he deserves," said the groom.

"Then," ejaculated Margaret, changing the tone of her voice, "I hope she will marry him: only, when she comes north, I shall go south."

"Oh!" cried Williams, with a groan, "I hope we shall have no missus here but the son of Bleddyn's wife."

"In that case, butler, you would like to be rid of the present master?" said Mills, coming from the fireplace, and sitting down, his arms lounging over the table. "I say, my old fellow, it is a pity we cannot give him one of those friendly chokes we gave the old dog the other day, to release him of his pain. But we must couple that M'Farlane along with him; we must send them bang out of the world in each other's claws. Lors, how jolly! Why, Margaret, we should come to life again! It would be like pouring salt water upon oysters; wouldn't it?"

"Hush! be quiet, Mills. I don't like to hear you use this language; master is our master," said Williams, with a grave gesture. "That tongue of yours will bring you into trouble, some of these days."

"And what matter if it does, now our poor missus is no more, and our young master is as good as dead to us? If he remains in England, we shan't see his face; if he goes out to India, he will catch the fever, or get a bullet through his head. I will let my tongue loose; and if I get into trouble, why that shan't trouble me. The deuce take it, if I can't fight my battles with these iron fists and straight understandings! Why, my old fellow, you may as well send me to the workhouse at once, and feed me on water-gruel."

"There he is! give me the lantern!" cried the groom, a moment afterwards, jumping up in a hurry as the hall-door bell rang. "Well, I am not sorry it is dark. I am sure, if I caught sight of Master Anarawd's face, I should not sleep a wink all night. Good lors! one feels a poke in the ribs when one thinks about him. How lonely he will feel to-night, Margaret!" he continued, lowering his voice. "It is a hard thing for a man to lose his mother!"

Margaret Morgan did not require being told that, for she had too recently been an eye-witness to scenes in the sick-chamber, and had been crying all day. When she went up to bed, and passed her mistress's door, a fresh paroxysm of grief seized her, and she could not close her eyes that night.

The next footstep that ascended the stairs, and passed near that lonely and deserted room, was that of a deeper mourner than Margaret. He hesitated, stopped : his hand was upon the door-handle ; he withdrew it, for she was gone! He groaned inwardly, moved to his own apartment and shut the door. It was best he should shut himself out from the world at a moment when intrusion would have newly barbed the arrows of grief.

While sitting at his breakfast on the following morning, his father entered. He looked dissipated, and having some papers in his hand, said—

"There!" throwing a letter from the Horse Guards upon the breakfast-table. "Your commission has arrived at last. You may thank God for it. The quicker you are off, the better. In the army there may be some chance for you."

Anarawd took up the letter, and read it in silence.

"Do not delay in getting through your examination. Gilford tells me there is no fear of your not passing, so that's all right. You will have to see about your outfit. I am off to Paris the moment I get to town. You had better ask Gilford to accompany you to Buckmaster. Don't let those knaves sack you, because you happen to be the son of a large landed proprietor. Do you hear?"

"Yes, sir."

"Well, what else have I to say? Ah, yes, this absurd attachment of yours, that your poor weak mother would encourage: it is the last time I intend to broach the subject. You shall hear first what I have to say, then, sir, you are at liberty to act as you please; only recollect things are now changed. It is of no importance to me, if you are fool enough to persist in shutting yourself out of property which would come to you at my death. I wish you to know I intend to marry again, and hope I may have sons who will be more after my own heart than my present son."

He paused, looked excited, and spoke with unusual rapidity. Though it was barely ten o'clock in the day, he had already taken several glasses of strong brandy-and-water.

Anarawd felt as if he were turning into stone. He could not withdraw his eyes from his father's fiery face, so sensual and bacchanalian-looking.

His father was embarrassed in turn, by eyes which seemed to be searching deeper into his thoughts than he liked. He, perhaps, felt for the moment that he had committed himself, and that it would have been more politic to have left the words unsaid. He, however, turned it off by saying—

"Ah! well, I suppose this is rather premature; mere random talk. What I have particularly to communicate to you is of a different nature : it is concerning Miss Lewis's birth."

Anarawd shrank at the words, and the cottage on the sea-shore rose before his mind like a spirit of evil.

" Oh, so you know already?"

" No; what is it you mean, sir?"

" No? Why, I thought you did: what the deuce made you turn so white, then?" He waited for an answer in vain, and continued—

" Why, it is all humbug, all a lie, about that girl being Lewis's legitimate child. The man has never been married. Lord Morlif has taken the trouble to learn particulars about him from his friends in Naples, and can prove this to be the case. A nice mess you have placed yourself in! I need not remind you that the affair as it now stands is ten times worse than it was before, and to expect any retractation on my part would be absurd. You may well look perplexed, and perhaps you will now come over to my thinking, that your fancy for marrying this Gertrude Lewis is an insult to society as well as your family. I am now your only remaining parent. Perhaps you will listen to my advice for the first and the last time. Mark what I say, hear me: if you marry that girl, she will be a curse to you. I have had about as much experience in these matters as any one, and know how and when to resist the fascinations of the fair sex. I know, too, how the feelings and passions fluctuate. You, whom I can look upon as a neophyte and nothing more, perhaps I ought rather to pity than condemn, particularly when I take into consideration the desultory education you have had, and the many disadvantages under which you have laboured. In the first place, you were a wretched, puny child, caused from over-care; you were afterwards allowed to run wild about the country, because a country practitioner said it would bring the colour back into your cheeks. Your mother believed this. Instead, therefore, of being knocked about in a public school, as you ought to have been, you were wasting your life here in getting into mischief, and into such scrapes as no child in the universe would have got into but yourself. Then came Mr. Gilford, who had the greatest difficulty to get you into training. The man had a pretty life of it, I believe. One day you would put him in a fume, and another into despair; he never had, for the first twelvemonth, a moment's peace; while he persisted in your mother's presence that you had a good share of genius, and that he did not despair of you. Then there was that stupid old antiquary, Mr. Maurice, who turned your head with British and Welsh history, and worthless old legends, doing you more harm, perhaps, with his absurd romantic nonsense than your mother's indulgences. I acknowledge that all this has been pernicious to your character; I am afraid it has thrown a shadow over your future prospects—that is, if you do not now make a grand effort to right yourself. Now is your opportunity; embrace it, and give up all ideas of having anything to do with Gertrude Lewis. Mind what I say; I repeat my warning, she will only be a clog to you, a bitter curse. I know too well how it will be when you enter the army and society: you will then perceive you are not in the position you should be. Instead of this young lady's being a helpmate through life, as your romantic ideas lead you to suppose, what if she should turn out to be your bane? You will then loathe the object you once cherished: it must and will end so; there is no help for it. Consider, for Heaven's sake, in this age who thinks of romance? who thinks of being faithful to his lady-love? The days of Troubadours, chivalry, and tournaments are gone by; rouse yourself to a sense of what is necessary for your good. Shake off this girl at once, and become a man; you have been a Simon Pure long enough—don't go on dreaming and imagining yourself a modern Troubadour or knight-errant, that thinks his salvation rests solely upon being constant to his first love. You think, perhaps, I am a little severe, and should have more regard for your feelings. No doubt, it is hard enough to obliterate ideas and opinions which have been instilled from early childhood. I have spoken, perhaps, at the wrong moment. When the lamb is crying for its dam, it wants a cordial, not a sermon. But time presses, I have no alternative."

Young Gwynne was standing leaning against the mantelpiece. Not a word rose to his lips while he was writhing under his father's heartless language. Mr. Gwynne continued—

" Unfortunately, your love for your mother has been your ruin; but her influence will not injure your advancement for the future. You are now going to be launched upon the world, sir—launched upon the world; and what will woman's precepts and nursery injunctions do for you there? I defy you to make any use of them They are as waste paper, sir, and nothing more. This is an age, as you will find, when man seeks to be independent; he must feel his way. Pray, sir, how is that way to be felt by you? Not by stopping at trifles—not by picking out scruples of conscience, like plums in a school-pudding. You will find that will not answer. Before you have been in the army a month, you will see I am right. I know you will smart under numberless annoyances, and lay yourself open to ridicule; you will be a target for all the young fellows in your regiment to pop at, while you will be longing to escape to Wales, your beloved Wales, like a truant school-boy. That will never do; you must emerge from this chrysalis state, and make up your mind to say good-bye to Wales, and all connected with it, for years to come. The life you have been leading here for the last twelvemonth, with your dogs, horses, fishing-rods, and your fair Dulcinea, is a pretty enough rustic picture. In these stirring days, pretty rustic pictures will not do; the fashion is gone, it was a perverted taste. We are all progressing, and have no longer a relish for walking with old Noah into his musty ark, or for keeping company with shepherdesses and milk-maids. No, young man, you have to learn the cry of the present day — Forward, forward! That must be your motto, and the motto of every young man entering upon life. What do you say to that, sir? am I not right?"

"Right in one sense of the word, sir; but there are two ways of going forward," replied Anarawd in a rigid tone; "and I hope to select that which will secure to me at least respect and esteem in this world."

"Hem! By this, you mean to infer I have forfeited the one and the other; and you have no intention to follow my advice.

There is little hope for you: thank God, Her Majesty is taking you off my hands."

Mr. Gwynne walked up and down the room, glancing occasionally at his son's wasted form and colourless face. For a moment he felt his bearing, as well as his words, had been a little too severe. Then he argued that he had spoken for his good. Upon the strength of this, he rang the bell and ordered some sherry. Anarawd was about to leave the room.

"Wait a moment; I have a good deal more to say to you." He turned round to face his son—

"Am I to understand, sir, this important news I have communicated will not alter your views respecting Miss Lewis? I can hardly suppose it possible you can be such an idiot as to think now of marrying that girl. Good Heavens! imagine the son of the old stock of Bleddyn bound by matrimony to one with a stigma upon her birth!

Have a sense of duty to your family, if you have not to yourself. Don't insult your ancestors. Talk of proper and high feelings! Never preach of that again! It is your duty, sir, and you ought to consider it your duty, to give her up at once. It is as well you should be reminded of your position; though, as I said before, it is of little importance to me. I will marry again."

Anarawd put his hand over his face, and, staggering forward, sank upon a chair. Williams at the moment came into the room with the wine, and saw at a glance that his young master was ill.

When he came to himself, the housekeeper, Williams, and Morgan were standing near him, with concern written in their faces. He was too confused at first to know what had happened to himself. He drank a glass of wine which the housekeeper offered him, and was better. Mr. Gwynne had disappeared.

Shortly afterwards, he got up and walked to his own study, when Morgan could not refrain from whispering to her companion—

"Is he not changed! I am glad my poor missus can't look at him—that I am."

The distressing news which had just been communicated to him was a greater blow, perhaps, than he was conscious of. At the moment, he was incapable of reasoning. He could only feel he must counter-order his horse, and send a note to Clogwyn, instead of going there himself. That day he would not see Gertrude, however much he might long to do so. He determined to remain closeted by himself, for he would not meet his father at dinner. He shuddered at the thought of going through the tedium of a meal alone in his company, where much state and ceremony were always observed. It was harrowing enough to hear that voice through the walls which divided them, talking to his agent in his noisy and unconcerned manner. One moment they were in the hall, then outside the house; Mr. M'Farlane walking upon his toes after his master, bowing to the ground at every fresh direction repeated to him. Both wore a suit of new black—how inappropriate to both! Various were the orders and injunctions given. Mr. Gwynne would have the drawing-room newly furnished, and another greenhouse built. The cottage near the wooden bridge should come down: Mr. M'Farlane was right, it was a disgrace to the estate. The sooner the little old woman was packed off to the workhouse, the better. She should not remain there to be his pensioner any longer. He had merely done that to oblige his lady, and now he saw the folly of it.

"Troubles never come alone," is a proverb in common use. That night was not to close before another painful scene occurred at Bleddyn, for which young Gwynne was not prepared.

Midnight approached, and he was sitting

before his fire, weighed down by thoughts which none could share, when he was suddenly roused to a sense of something going on in the house. Footsteps were crossing and recrossing the hall. Some smothered sounds occasionally caught his ear. He started up. What could it be? Fire, perhaps: no, that was his father's voice. Again he listened; he could not be mistaken. The brandy and the sherry had been in request all day, and were now taking effect. How horrible it was!

He sat down again with a fresh feeling of wretchedness, resolved to keep away from so painful and disgusting a sight. But it was not to be; a knock came to the door, and then Jones entered.

"Please, sir, I am sorry, but we can do nothing with master to-night. Williams, Mills, and myself have been trying this hour or more to get him to bed. We can't do it. You never saw such a state as he is in! Will you please, sir, to come to him?"

Mr. Gwynne was in the dining-room; the decanters and the dessert still standing upon the table. Anarawd followed Jones immediately, and found his father standing upon the hearth-rug. His face was mottled. His coat and neckcloth were off; his hair was rough and entangled, and his eyes glaring like those of a madman.

The sight of his son seemed to increase his disordered state. He shook his fists at him, and ground his teeth, crying—

"Get out of my sight! I don't want your hawk's-eyes here! Get out of the house, you puny fellow! you have no business here; you have sold your birthright—ay, sold it for a worse thing than a pot of broth. Go, you fool, or I will throw the chair at your head. Don't come near me! Do you hear? do you not hear?"

He began tearing his hair, and bawling in a loud tone—

"I will shoot you all if you come a step

nearer, or dare to talk to me. You are all fools and asses!"

On a sudden his face and manner changed; and lowering his voice into a whining, peevish tone, he continued—

"There, there, do you see her? she is coming to torment me, to tell me I have treated her ill! I didn't treat her ill, I didn't. Keep her away, keep her away from me! I never treated her ill!"

"You had better come to bed, sir; you will be better in bed," said Anarawd, in as soothing a tone as he could command.

"Bed, bed! Hold your tongue, you fool, or I will bed you—tie you to the bed-post! Am I an infant, and you Mrs. Gamp? I am not going to bed at your beck. Go, you fool, go away! Confound those eyes of yours! keep them off me! There, there—she is coming again! Keep her away, keep her away! I didn't treat her ill—I never did treat her ill! Bring me more brandy;

more brandy, brandy—I will have more brandy!"

His irritability seemed to increase, and became frightful to witness.

"The brandy is killing you, sir—don't touch it; don't give it him, Williams," said Anarawd, laying his hand upon his father's arm and speaking authoritatively.

Mr. Gwynne, with a yell, flung him off with violence, and seizing one of the decanters, hurled it at his son's head.

"I tell you what, sir," said Mills, coming forward with a determination to subdue his master, whatever the consequence might be; "it is no use, sir, your going on in this way: if you won't let us take you off quietly to bed, we shall have to put you in a strait-waistcoat. As sure as I am living, we will do it too! Here, Williams and Jones, give me a helping hand."

Mr. Gwynne was cowed in an instant on seeing the stern determination of Mills. They carried him to his chamber at once, almost without a struggle. There, when he saw himself reflected in the high cheval-glass, he put himself into a pugilistic attitude, and splintered the glass with his clenched fists.

Returning to his own room, Anarawd for some time stood upon the hearth, watching the dying embers, grief-stricken, and repeating in a half-absent way—

" Forward ! indeed this is going ' forward !' It is the road to destruction. Who that cared for his own soul, his own reputation, would follow my father's advice, or take his motto, ' Forward,' with such perverted views ? To witness such degradation is loathsome to me ! Enough !" He raised his hand to his head as if in pain. " I can endure this state of things no longer. To be three days with him, and witness repetitions of such a day and scene as this, would make me lose my senses. These are trials indeed—God help me, and give me strength to bear them !"

He took a knapsack, packed it, swung it over his shoulders, took his cap and his purse, and descended the staircase, stopping first for a moment before his mother's silent and solitary chamber.

The servants were all in bed, and the home seemed strangely quiet. He repaired to the breakfast-room, where the windows opened to the ground, and having unfastened the shutters with as quiet a hand as possible, he passed out.

It was a piercing cold night; black clouds hung in gloomy patches over the mountain-tops, and the snow had but partly melted in the valleys. There could not have been a more dreary aspect over the face of Nature than she at that moment presented.

As he passed through the gate which led to the hills at the back of the mansion, something glided across his path. It was gone in an instant, and all was quiet again. It startled him, although, perhaps, no more than a timid hare. He was unnerved, and the slightest surprise had an effect upon his frame. His mind was not there. " Was Gertrude, his beloved Gertrude, the only comfort left to him in the world—was she really illegitimate? That soft little hand always nestling into his, thus warming his heart when other things failed; those gentle, loving eyes reading his thoughts and responding to them; could she bring disgrace upon his house? He would endure a thousand trials and evils, sooner than that this stigma should attach to one so mingled with his existence. Their hearts were one; he had returned to find her more devoted and more confiding than ever. To wrench her from his heart now would be impossible. He was thankful his mother had not known this distressing circumstance. She had said, ' Do not forsake her, do not break her heart!' Perhaps she had a foreshadowing of this evil. The warning was given him to prevent him from yielding to the exacting duty that was ready to sweep all before it, and make his heart bankrupt. Yet, why should he let this weigh upon his heart? why make himself miserable? Gertrude herself was pure; she was free from blame, if her parents had not been so. Why should her ill-birth blast her in the sight of the world? What would the world's censure be in such a case but one of its ten thousand absurdities!"

He strode on through the gloomy fog. "Was this false argument, was the fault of those censurable to be visited upon the innocent? Still, it was a stigma upon her he loved, which could not be effaced. Alas for his poor ill-fated Gertrude! Was he, then, to desert her? Never! On the contrary, he would be more to her than before; he would shield her, and raise her from her misfortune. It should be no blight to her existence, so far as he was concerned; even the secret, if in his power to hide it, she should never know. There should be no change in himself. Yet," again the words came upon his lips, and he repeated—" Illegitimate."

Hail was beating in his face, and as he ascended the hill, the blast grew colder, roaring among the crags; fragments of rocks were loosened, and fell near his feet, threatening destruction to everything in their path. Still he continued his route, apparently careless of the inclemency of the weather or the dangers that environed him.

When the mind is overburdened or oppressed with sorrow, how man lives within himself, and how outward discomforts vanish, although at another moment they would be heavily felt!

Three days Anarawd wandered among the Carnarvonshire hills, resting at night in some small inn by the road-side, there despatching letters to Gertrude, to relieve her anxiety about his position. The people observed him with not a little curiosity, travelling alone in such weather in mid winter. What could be his motive? The small parlours, too, at the inns were cold, musty, and damp. The tourists having ceased to visit the country, the rooms had been shut up for the winter, and were cheerless. On that account, perhaps, they were more congenial to the wanderer's desolate feelings.

Having rested one night at Llanberis, he started at an early hour to walk through the pass on his way home. Icicles were hanging like colossal pillars from the projecting crags, high above the road, and sheets of ribbed and mottled ice covered the fields and glades in patches, all the way between him and the white crested heights of Snowdon. The mountain queen was but partly enveloped in her sable mantle: all was awful silence. Never had Anarawd remembered to have seen her with so unfriendly a face; not a ray of light illuminated any of her features, but every part looked black, purple, or white, with cold, and withered with age. The streams, half frozen, interlining the declivities, and a few stray sheep sheltering under the cliffs, looking disconsolate enough upon the solitary stranger, were all discoverable in the dreary waste before him.

The waterfalls exhibited grottoes of ice, which were to be seen at their feet, formed by the splashing of the spray, freezing as it fell over the roots of trees and stones. It was interesting and curious to examine these beauteous works of frost, fairy castles soon to melt away like dreams of early childhood. The wanderer continued on his route, momentarily diverted from his cares by these objects, but too soon returning to them again.

It was midnight when he reached Bleddyn. Williams was sitting up for him.

" I am thankful to see your face again, sir !". ejaculated the old butler, the moment the door was opened, and his young master stood before him. " Indeed, Master Anarawd, by keeping away you have made us all miserable. Every night I have been sitting up for you. We wondered what had become of you."

" Indeed, Williams, I am sorry."

" Never mind, now you are safe, sir. I

was only afraid something had happened, knowing how much trouble you have upon your mind."

Tears were in the old man's eyes, as he looked anxiously in his young master's face.

"I am grieved. Why did you not go to Clogwyn? they would have told you there I was safe."

"No, that we could not do, sir; master has been in such a temper. He swore, and said not one of us should go from here to Clogwyn."

"When did your master go?"

"This morning. Most of the servants have gone by the same train. Master told me I was to go too, but I begged hard to remain till you left the country."

"Thank you, Williams; I like to have you with me to the last. We shall soon have to part for many a long day; perhaps for ever!"

"Don't say that, sir. Dear heart alive, how wet you are! Pray, Master Anarawd, change your clothes; you will find everything in your room ready."

The knapsack was taken off, and he went to his room.

Half an hour later, he was lounging in his own easy chair, greatly refreshed by his change of habiliments.

As the butler arranged the supper upon the table, he said—

"Nelly of the Bridge, sir, has been inquiring for you. They are going to turn her out of her cottage; she wants you to speak to master."

"That shall not be," replied young Gwynne, with a look of dissatisfaction. "Tell Mr. M'Farlane I want to see him in the morning: don't forget."

"The poor old woman is broken-hearted."

Anarawd remained silent, and the butler left him.

The old spaniel was sitting upon his haunches upon the hearth, wagging his tail, and looking happy at his master's return, and wishing to attract his attention.

"So you want me to take notice of you, poor old fellow," said Anarawd, stretching out his hand and patting him upon the head. "You are overjoyed at having me home again, are you not? in your way giving me a welcome. It will be the last time, perhaps, I shall ever receive your welcome."

The old dog raised his paws and rested them upon his young master's knee, while Anarawd continued—

"And good old Williams, with his kind anxious face, has also given me a welcome. It is pleasant to be thus received by a faithful servant and a faithful dog, in such a cold world as this."

CHAPTER X.

Winter is over; the snow and ice have disappeared, and the rude blustering equinoctial gales have swept over the country. Primroses, blue-bells, and the wood-anemones checker the green banks with their welcome bloom. The birds are singing in the woods, the bees humming in the air; the gardeners busy with their flowers, and the farmers with their land. Nature smiles sweetly and softly; all is cheerful now; she is roused from her wintry sleep. The common mother holds out her hand and welcomes all her progeny—youth and age, rich and poor; all animal and vegetable life revives. Man arouses from his wintry thoughts to review the world with a more charitable and contented spirit. Even the invalid revives in the warm rays of the sun, and hope's fairy dreams once more deceive the heart. Spring is universally welcomed. The Sunday citizen population with eagerness turns pedestrian, and hurries forward to the fields to enjoy sweet Nature, unalloyed and unspoiled by art.

It was at this genial season that Gertrude Lewis's spirit shared in the general elevation. The preceding three months had been to her a period of gloom and dreariness. She had been alone in a large house, separated from those nearest her heart, and in mourning for one who could return to her no more. A month after Anarawd Gwynne had left, he returned to Wales for a week, previous to joining his regiment in Scotland. This had been the only break in her solitariness from that time to the present.

She was in the greenhouse, ordering the

gardener to collect some choice flowers just then in blossom, and to take them to the library, where they were to be arranged. One camellia, clustered with bloom, was to be placed upon the ebony table, opposite to the beautiful bust. Everything looked in exquisite order, and the house had undergone a thorough cleaning. Gertrude, too, had a Spring smile upon her face. There was a lightness about her step as she moved from room to room, a sure indication that some one was expected who was of interest to herself. It was to her one of her brightest Spring days, from feeling that her being was in harmony with Nature.

She had taken off her black dress and robed herself in pure white, for time was rapidly passing. Every moment, like a little white cloud, she was floating about the room, and going to the window to look down the drive, and catch, if possible, a glimpse of those she expected, through the trees. Again her little fingers were rearranging some of the ornaments, and giving the finishing stroke to everything in the room. Would it strike him as pretty and comfortable on his first entrance? would he be pleased? The flowers looked lovely, and the mosses so fresh about the flower-pots, and a sun-gleam lighted up his treasure of a picture. If he would but come now, this moment the effect would be charming, and first impressions are everything. She laughed to herself. " I should not wonder if all my labour is thrown away upon him. He will be more engrossed with me, and shall I not be so with him? Yes, dear, darling papa, here he comes!" She sprang into the hall, and was soon locked in his arms.

Ricardo Lewis was a man of strong affection, with a good deal of foreign and somewhat combustible blood in his veins. He could not meet events in the calm, phlegmatic manner which is so characteristic of an Englishman. Here, though not in everything, he was a thorough native of the warm South. We shall not be surprised, on entering the library two or three hours later in the evening, to find him still in an excited state, Gertrude upon his knee, and his arm around her. Not till now had he noticed how charmingly pretty and comfortable everything appeared. He suddenly exclaimed—

"Oh, my darling child! you can have no conception how happy I am to be at home again. After knocking about in the world, and meeting with so much roughness, you appear such a contrast, my gentle Gertrude! What delight it is to fold you in my arms! This taste displayed, too—it is like coming back into Paradise. To possess the wealth of Peru, I would never leave you again. I could live upon the Clogwyn with my little girl for a hundred years, and never wish a change."

"A hundred years is a long time, papa," said Gertrude, laughing. "What a shrivelled little old woman I should have grown into by that time! and you with a white beard looking like a patriarch. You know, dear papa, if we did not seek for change, we should have it all the same.—Oh, that cruel word, 'change!'"

"But our hearts, Gertrude, they would not be changed. They would not wither, if our faces did."

"No, no, dearest papa."

"That was a strange smile, Gertrude, and the 'No, no,' so faint."

"It is your fancy. I did not mean it to be faint: I am so happy to have you home. Don't talk of the future, nor think about hearts changing: parents' and children's hearts can hardly change — can they, papa?"

"You sometimes hear of such things," replied Captain Lewis, with his brow slightly contracted. "Let me look at that dear little face again. Why do you turn it away, Gertrude? You have grown thinner; your cheeks are not half the size they were.

This colour in your cheeks is from excitement, not health. What have they been doing with you? I hope the great folks at Bleddyn have not spoiled my Gertrude, and made her dissatisfied with her home. That would be a heavy sorrow to me."

" Do not imagine such a thing, dear papa. You must recollect I have had much to try me since you left. Your leaving me was a trial, and dear Lady Elizabeth's death has weighed much upon my spirits. Had you known her, and seen us together, you would better understand what a friend I have lost in losing her. To learn ill from her would have been impossible."

" Yes, my dear Gertrude, I am ready to admit you have had enough to depress you; your living so much alone has been distressing to me. From the time I heard of poor Mrs. Parry's death, I have been miserable about you. Why did you not write to your governess to come to you, as I proposed?"

" I did. She has been in great trouble, and could not leave her home."

"Time must indeed have hung heavily. You have been quite alone ever since Lady Elizabeth's death?"

"Yes."

"How did you employ yourself in your solitude? Have you made any progress with your studies?"

"The last three months I have been hard at work to kill time and blunt sorrow, dear papa."

"I reproach myself sorely for having left you as I did. I have come home now, never to leave you again. We will shut out sorrow, and be as happy as we were before; shall we not, my dearest Gertrude?"

"I hope so; but sorrow will not always be shut out."

"This is not like my laughing little Gertrude. You look so serious, too. A moment since, you said you did not wish to look into the future; why look back? 'Look not mournfully into the past—it comes not back again," Longfellow says.

You are allowing the past still to prey upon your spirits. Remember that mourning for your friend will not restore her to you. Come, let me have a happy face to-night; at least, to-night; or I shall feel I have hardly had my full share of welcome."

"Pray don't say that. My heart is overflowing with feelings of joy. If not sufficiently demonstrative, they are still in my heart. Believe me, dear papa."

He kissed her, and was silent for a few minutes.

"How long did you say you were at Bleddyn?"

"Three months."

"Three months? were you there all that time?"

"Yes; and I have only to regret my visit ended so sadly."

"How came Gwynne to allow you to be so much with his lady? You are aware how high the family carry themselves;

they are not intimate with any family in the neighbourhood. And, above all things, I am surprised that he should receive a daughter of mine under his roof."

" He did not, I think, sanction my going there with any good-will; but somehow fortune favoured me. It would have been wanting in politeness in him to have treated me otherwise. But there is not much friendship lost between us."

" You don't like him, then?"

" No; he is no favourite."

" He can make himself extremely agreeable."

" That sort of agreeableness does not please me, papa. I have a particular dislike to an over-courteous address: there is an insincerity, as well as an absence of nature, about it. Few of the gentlemen I met at Bleddyn had what I considered agreeable manners; but I am thought fastidious."

" This long dreary year that I have

passed has been an epoch in your life, my little Gertrude. Most of your time seems to have been spent at Bleddyn: of course you have seen a great deal of company?"

"Yes, papa; after the first two or three months the house was full of visitors, and Lady Elizabeth would always have me there."

There was a pause.

"Well, Gertrude, after this short experience, is the world as bright as you expected? Have you found any black spots in it?"

Gertrude gave a little start: whether it was from the odd expression of his face, or his words, she hardly knew, and with a hurried manner she replied—

"It is not all sunshine: that does not belong to the high and the wealthy, any more than to the cottager. As to a black spot or two, I don't quite understand you: I should be afraid there were many more black spots than bright ones, if you mean what I do."

"You have not discovered any one in particular?"

"No, papa; I think not."

"You hesitate, Gertrude: you admit, too, there are more clouds than sunshine. Does not that infer you have been more unhappy than happy since I have been absent? Is not that what you mean?"

"Yes, dear papa; but don't ask me these odd questions. I want to think only of you to-night. It is such joy to have you with me again—to see you and to hear your voice! You cannot tell how I have longed for this day!"

She threw one arm round his neck, and laid her cheek upon his soft dark beard, as it had been her custom to do from a child, and relapsed into silence.

Captain Lewis put his hand upon her cheek and pressed her to him. "Bless you, my dearest Gertrude! after all, it is worth while to go to the other end of the globe to feel this delightful reaction of happiness. One little thing in the world cares for me—loves me. Absence has not weakened that love; has it, dearest?"

"No, dear papa, I hope not."

"Why do you say 'hope not?' are you not quite sure?"

"Yes, quite sure. Love planted in the heart of a child must live there for ever. Why doubt that it can change, papa?"

"Gertrude!"

"Well, dearest papa?"

Gertrude did not see the strange expression which came over Captain Lewis's face, nor observe that his eye was resting upon her hand, which he had laid upon his palm.

"What makes your hand twitch in that nervous way?"

"I did not know anything was the matter with it." She drew it gently away and hid it in the folds of her dress. "I suppose I am excited from seeing you, dear papa, after being so long quiet; and not being very strong, it affects my nerves: that's all."

The instant the words had passed her lips, she felt she had not quite spoken the truth. Her father's words and manner had agitated her. She was thinking about Anarawd, and longing to open her heart to him, and to make a general confession of all that happened to her in his absence. She knew she could not feel at ease as long as she kept him in ignorance of her engagement, yet she wanted the courage to disclose it to him. The dreaded day must be deferred. She would wait till Anarawd's letter came—that would give her an outlet: so she reasoned. Many, like Gertrude, would have felt it was an embarrassing position. She had no kind friend to intercede for her. The prop and the hope she had once looked to was no more. She reflected how difficult it would be to convince her father, that her love for the heir of Bleddyn did not diminish her love for him. It was a new affection which had sprung up in her heart, quite distinct in its nature from every other feeling. She cared for her father as much as if she had never been intimate with Anarawd Gwynne. Though she was ready to acknowledge, when her father was away, that she had been haunted with fears lest her affection for her lover had weaned her in some degree from him, now she was again in his presence, and felt his influence, every feeling of her preceding doubt vanished. Her love for her parent was as deep and earnest as ever. What was that overpowering pleasure she experienced at his return, but a sure proof that there was no diminution of her affection? Such a conviction, in the midst of all her uneasiness, was at least a comfort.

While these thoughts were passing in her mind, Captain Lewis was calmly looking upon her face, and admiring her as if she had been a picture or a fine piece of sculpture. She was no longer the little Hebe he had left, with the full bloom of health upon her cheeks; but her features were improved, and the delicate whiteness of her skin was dazzling. She was the only being in the world who shared his heart and his ample fortune. How privileged he was to possess a home with such a being, and to have such a welcome as he had from those lips! Why, then, had he a doubt that his beloved child was not all to him, as she had been before, and he to her? It was but a foolish passing thought.

He then began to recall her early years, when she was a tiny engaging little thing, clinging to his neck as he paraded the deck of his ship, with her small fingers twisting his hair and whispering affection into his ear. She had said right; her love for him had taken root early in her heart, and for that reason could know no change. Why, then, did any tormenting thoughts hover about his brain? It was because his heart was tainted with jealousy: he was jealous that Lady Elizabeth had won her affection; and he was afraid others might also have influenced her in other ways. He could never support an interference between him and his child's affection. He would shut her out from the world, and keep her to himself. Perhaps this was selfish, but how could he help himself? were not all his thoughts centred in her, and was she not wrapped up in his heart? He had watched tenderly over her early years, and had superintended her education. Nothing on his part had been neglected, nothing spared to give her joy— wholesome joy, and to mature the cultivation of her mind. That culminating moment had arrived. She had thriven under his care and solicitude, and she did him full justice in both. She was gentle in manner, as well as in voice, and free from all affectation, which was a great charm; she had a quick, sound judgment, and was in every way a delightful and joyous companion. She was precisely the child after his own heart. Had he not, then, every reason to be proud of her, and to be jealous, too, if there was cause for it? Jealousy, he was ready to admit, was a dark passion; yet in him it might be excused. He had a right to be jealous, and a right to keep her to himself. If it were indeed selfish, he would still keep her to himself.

By the knitting of his brow, and his hurried manner in breaking the silence, it is doubtful if he were quite satisfied with the conclusion at which he had arrived.

"Well, my little Gertrude, what a pause there has been! You have not told me how they are going on at Angharad. Is the school thriving?"

"Not very well, I am afraid: there has been a disturbance between the master and boys. The village has not been quiet, either: they say there are a drunken set there, doing much harm."

"I am sorry to hear this: drunkenness is a fearful failing in this country, and it seems to get worse instead of better. They need occupation for the mind. What are the poor fellows to do? It is not to be expected they can go on day after day, out of their beds into the ploughed fields, and back again into their beds. No, Gertrude; man requires some relaxation from toil. He cannot live without it. The consequence is, when he cannot obtain a wholesome pleasure, he runs foolishly into an unwholesome one. Now, I know from some experience, these Welsh fellows, taking them *en masse*, are more active in mind than in body; and if their taste for letters were encouraged, they would find mental enjoyment, instead of seeking that excitement in drink which is offered to them by the public-houses at every turn and corner in the streets. As affairs are at the present moment, it is lamentable. I would have done a great deal for them if they would have let me, or rather if Mr. Gwynne had not put a clog to the wheel whenever I made the attempt. That poor village might easily be reformed, with its well-meaning inhabitants, were they put into better training, and more noticed by the influential in the county."

Gertrude thought how much her father's views corresponded with Anarawd's. He was always talking of and grieving over his beer-drinking country, as he designated it; but, with all its faults, he loved it still. He was devoted to Wales, and anxious for its welfare. If her father could only know his character truly, he would be reconciled to him; they would be friends, and the country would benefit by their united exertions. She did not dare to breathe to her father what her reflections were; the mere mentioning of Anarawd Gwynne's name would rouse that suspicion which she particularly wished at the moment to avoid.

This conversation was brought to a close by the entrance of a footman with refreshments. A few days after, Ricardo Lewis was again sitting with Gertrude, looking over her sketch-book. He appeared pleased with his pupil's progress in drawing.

"How improved you are, Gertrude! It is ridiculous for me to think of giving you any more instruction; you have greater execution than I ever had, when I was in more practice. You have put an extinguisher upon my training. I will take you to London, purposely to visit the exhibitions this year. I understand there are some prime pictures, quite worth a journey to town. You could then have some lessons, if you would like them."

" That would be charming!"

" Then you would enjoy the trip?"

" Yes, I think so indeed, papa."

" In that case it is settled. We will run up for a month before the season closes. The change, too, I think, would do you good."

She thanked him with a kiss. A few minutes afterwards, putting away her sketches, she said, in an unusually nervous manner—

" Those sketches, papa, remind me that I have not yet told you what I am fearful will cause you much annoyance. If I am to blame, I still hope for forgiveness, as it was done in ignorance. I was not aware, when

Lord Morlif first came into the country, that you had ever been acquainted with him, and that you were not now on good terms."

" Gertrude! what are you talking about? Lord Morlif! You don't mean to say that infamous, lying villain—that base reptile—has been in this country during my absence?"

" Yes, papa, he took Bryn-y-Coed during the summer months—but pray don't be so excited," said Gertrude, with a half-palsied voice.

" Good heavens! don't, Gertrude, tell me that you have had anything to do with that man—that you have been in his company?"

" I have, dear papa, I am sorry to say. I met him frequently at Bleddyn: and he has often been to Clogwyn, too."

" Here, in my house, Gertrude? His pertinacious impudence! his meanness, his cowardice, to take this advantage when I was from home! Had I been here, he would have skulked away from me like a cowardly hound. The demon!"

"Dearest papa, do be calm." She pressed his hand between her own, and looked pleadingly in his face. "Do not be angry, nor use this language; it is unlike you. Base as Lord Morlif is, and much as he strove to make mischief between you and me, there has no real harm been done, believe me."

"Mischief! the reptile! and you sat and listened to his lying tongue, instead of flying from that miscreant? Oh! Gertrude, I have been a fool indeed to leave you! What was Mrs. Parry about, to sanction any one like him entering my doors in my absence? Gertrude, that villain has once had a horse-whipping from me. Had I come in contact with him, I would, as sure as heaven, have beaten his breath out of his body."

He pushed Gertrude away from him, and threw himself back in his chair, his lips quivering with rage. His companion was terrified: she had never before seen him in a passion, and was bewildered. Some moments elapsed before he spoke, and then it was in a harsh, quick way.

"Let me hear, Gertrude, what his mendacious tongue has been telling you. What is this mischief he has been attempting? Speak; I will have no concealment: there is no knowing what his false lips might fabricate."

Gertrude shrank from her father's harsh words, and burst into tears. She said she was ready to tell him everything, and only entreated him not to be angry with her. Lord Morlif had caused her great uneasiness on account of what he had stated about him—she was miserable.

Captain Lewis was calm in a moment, while his face turned pale. "Come here, my child," said he, in a subdued tone—he held out his hand, and drew her to him. "It is a sad thing to give way to temper. I have been harsh, but you will forgive me. You are not to blame, my poor child! I have done foolishly to keep you in ignorance of our family secrets; yet, God knows, my motive was a good one. I was anxious to keep you as much as possible in ignorance of the sins which destroy the peace of this world. I thought it better not to unveil a sad history attached to our family. Did Lord Morlif come into this room?"

" He did."

" And that portrait, did he observe it?"

Gertrude immediately described the scene which had taken place in the library, and mentioned other particulars. "He is not lost, then, to all feeling," was Captain Lewis's remark, and for some minutes he sat musing in silence. He then asked Gertrude what he had been saying of him that had made her miserable.

The question, though spoken in the calmest tones, was accompanied by so stern an expression of face, that Gertrude again felt her courage fail her. He had to repeat his words before she ventured to tell him how Lord Morlif had taken every opportunity to persuade her that her father had deceived her; that her mother was alive, and that he had ill-treated her. This, she knew, must be false; he could never have spoken so seriously of her mother's death, had he known she was alive. It was false; he could not deceive her, his own child.

In repeating the last sentence, her eye was fixed upon her father's colourless features, that would scarcely bear scrutiny. Captain Lewis immediately changed his posture by drawing her closer to him, and placing his hand upon her cheek. He could stand anything, but not her scrutiny. After a pause, he said gravely, "Gertrude, have you ever had reason to doubt my veracity?"

"Never, dear papa; nor do I doubt it now."

"I take Heaven as my witness that this accusation brought against me is a wicked falsehood. Your mother died when you were scarcely three years old. Yarico can be summoned to confirm what I state."

Gertrude looked up at him with her

innocent face beaming with renewed confidence. "Though these reports did make me unhappy, I could not bring myself to believe that you were deceiving me. One naturally shrinks from deception."

With something approaching nervousness, her father continued stroking her cheek, his hand occasionally concealing her face from his.

"What else, Gertrude, did that man tell you?"

"It pains you, dear papa; perhaps it had better remain untold."

With a slight movement of impatience, he requested her to proceed. Gertrude continued—

"He constantly hinted that there was something the matter with my mother; mentally or physically I was left to imagine, for he refused to clear up the mystery. One thought clung to my mind with cruel pertinacity—that she was deranged. You know in this particular I had ground to fear, dear papa, that there might be some truth in what he said. You have ever avoided speaking to me of my mother, and checked me invariably when I have broached the subject. I hope it was not the case; still, if she were thus afflicted, do not conceal it any longer from me. Let me hear the truth, however painful."

"That man is an atrocious villain. It requires self-command to sit calmly and listen to his villanies. There was nothing whatever the matter with your mother. She was an amiable and an exemplary woman. Australia did not agree with her; the climate impaired her health. She did not live to return to her own country. These are facts. What that man's motive could be for exciting you in this cruel way, Heaven only knows."

"What countrywoman was she, papa?"

"English. You are not unlike her; she had precisely the same coloured hair as your own."

"I am rejoiced to hear all this: that thought will not haunt me any more."

"It was a painful thought to brood over in your solitude. I need not wonder at your altered appearance. I will never forgive myself for going to Australia, and leaving you unprotected—never, Gertrude."

He rose hastily from his chair, and observed hurriedly—

"Let us go upon the terrace; I will smoke a cigar. Though the night is mild, still wrap yourself up well. I must take double care of my precious child, having treated her so ill. From the period you were left without your mother, under my charge, this is the first time I have neglected you."

"We won't call it neglect, dear papa; do not make yourself unhappy about it."

They passed into the garden, and for some time walked upon the terrace without either of them speaking.

"Gertrude," he at length resumed, "I must ask straightforward questions. Tell me if that villain Morlif paid you marked attention; and have you any idea yourself what his motives were for making me appear a deceiver in your eyes?"

Gertrude lowered her voice. " I have a great deal to tell you, dear papa, which will distress you."

She gave him the full particulars of what had transpired between herself and Lord Morlif. She also spoke of her obligations to Lady Elizabeth, and how she rejoiced when the Morlifs left the country.

" I cannot describe, Gertrude, how this information pains me — enrages me. I frighten you when I go into a passion; with a great effort I keep my indignation boiling within. Would that Morlif were within my reach! Yet it is, perhaps, well that he is not, for as sure as there is light in heaven I would take his life. The mean dastard!"

He strode rapidly before his companion, then hastily returned and held Gertrude in his arms. " You are not glossing over his infamy—you are not concealing anything from me—you are sure, Gertrude?"

"To the best of my recollection I have told you all. It is bad enough, surely, dear papa."

"He is a fiend," parenthesized Captain Lewis, once more pacing the terrace in silence.

Suddenly he stood before Gertrude, and again addressed her—

"As affairs have come to this, you shall know the extent of injury I have received at that man's hand. In recalling those painful details, and coupling them with his present atrocious conduct, I am almost unfitted for the task; yet, I will endeavour to clear up that mystery to you. Would it were in my power to bring him before the public! That picture in the library, Gertrude, that has so often excited your curiosity, is the portrait of my sister—my only sister. From children we were deeply attached. After my grandfather died, we went to live at Naples; and she was just in the prime of her beauty, attracting general attention. Seldom have I seen a more lovely woman than my poor sister. Her beauty was her misfortune, I will not say her shame. No, unhappy, luckless girl, she was an object of real pity. I never dwell upon her memory without a bitter pang.

"My first acquaintance with Lord Morlif was in Paris. Gwynne, with whom I was then intimate, introduced us, and I saw him frequently. Our next meeting was in Wales, then in Naples. Just a twelvemonth after we had settled there, I happened one day to meet him in the street, when in company with my sister. From that time an intimacy sprang up between them. I was then on the point of starting for Wales; but, previous to my departure, I warned my sister against him. I did not admire his character; but little did I know, at that time, how thoroughly unprincipled he was, or I should never have left home. It is a long story, Gertrude; I will epitomise as much as possible. When I returned to Naples, imagine my distress of mind on discovering that, in my absence, that wretch had gained my sister's affections—had changed her character, made her quarrel with her family, and had her completely under his influence. It was in vain that my mother and myself pointed out to her the little chance of happiness there was in marrying a man without principle and above her own sphere in life. She neither heeded our counsel nor our entreaties. The full extent of misery that man entailed upon our family can never be described. Where there had always been peace and harmony, there was soon nothing but bitterness and disagreement. My sister married him, and they went to France. Shortly after that event I sailed for Australia. It was remarkable, that when I landed in that country I became acquainted with a young man whom you have often heard me mention, Fitzhammond. He was intimate with the Morlifs, and, to my horror, he one day mentioned that Lord Morlif had married before he was twenty, was separated from his wife, and that there were three children, who lived with her in England. It was a great shock to me as you may suppose. I did not communicate this painful intelligence to my family, but kept my secret till my return from the New World. The moment I was in Europe, I never rested till I had found my poor sister and punished that scoundrel. He was in Paris, and my sister in Brussels. He had grown tired of his toy, and, without the slightest compunction, disclosed to her that he was a married man. The state of depression in which I found my poor sister was truly distressing. Broken-hearted, she returned home with me to die, a victim to that man's villany. Shortly afterwards my mother sickened and died, and I was left without a friend or family tie, save my little Gertrude. You are now in possession of my family secrets. You will own I have reason to feel a bitter enmity and repugnance towards Morlif. He was a curse to our family, and I cannot be too thankful that, through Lady Elizabeth's kindness, you are safe."

CHAPTER XI.

THE consciousness of secrecy where there should be candour, often preys upon the spirits. On the pillow at night, still undivulged, and again in the morning, that consciousness is present, and to exclude it is a vain attempt. We supplicate forgetfulness of it to no purpose. The only means of its removal a species of moral cowardice prevents, by asserting its power over reason.

Thus Gertrude day after day delayed opening her heart to her parent. Delay only enhanced the difficulty. The deception she maintained to shield her secret made the matter worse. In a state of mind miserable from this cause, she accompanied her father to London. They remained there but a short time, from his becoming indisposed, and being forced, in consequence, to return home earlier than they originally intended.

Gertrude began to feel uneasy about her father. He appeared depressed in spirits, at times, without any definable cause. She noticed a considerable change in his manner, which he tried to pass off by attributing it to the change of climate affecting his health, giving her hopes he should soon be better. Willingly would she have assented to the plea; but weeks elapsed, and still there was no amendment. He became solitary, and often in Gertrude's presence remained unusually silent. Documents, papers, and letters were left upon his table unopened; and he seldom, as had been his previous custom, read for amusement, or took any interest in the improvements of his estate.

It was a lovely evening in June. Lewis was in his garden, walking in the shade without his hat. Dissatisfied with his cigar, he had flung it away, dealing with it as he did at the moment with everything else. He stopped suddenly before a patch of garden-ground full of weeds, and overgrown flowers. It had once belonged to Gertrude, when she was a child. The spiders were spinning their cords from flower to flower among the rank grass, now growing so high that the blossoms could only peep out of the thick green mass which environed them. How desolate it appeared! There lay the little hoe and rake against a tree, spotted and discoloured by the weather; like the garden, neglected. It was not thus when Gertrude was a child. What would he not have given, were she but a child again! The remembrance of the time when she was placed under his protection, a little innocent, helpless creature, rose vividly before his mind. They had long lived in peace together; could they only have lived so still, their state unchanged, he would have been contented, and his secret might have gone with him to the grave. He had ever been solicitous that Gertrude should not have a want or a regret. If it could only continue as it had been, he being all to her, and she to him! He lamented he had gone to London, and dreaded the presentiment that had become a fixture in his mind.

Again he paraded the long walk, and stood facing the little garden-wilderness, deep in contemplation. Suddenly stooping, he gathered some of the flowers, and disentangling them from the weeds, folded them carefully in a letter and hurried to his library.

For above an hour he sat near the window, the ocean before him, talking at intervals to himself.

"Could I but shake off this incubus! Why should time lag as it does? I would not have you know, my dear Gertrude, how much I am suffering on your account! Had I foreseen events, I should have pursued another course of action. Heaven avert this misfortune from me! Let these foreshadowings go as they came, and leave my path unclouded! Oh! Gertrude, Gertrude, bitter indeed would be my lot should it be otherwise!"

He had scarcely ceased to soliloquize, when the door softly opened, and Gertrude in her riding attire entered.

"I am ready now, dearest papa. The horses are at the door. Come; the evening is lovely."

Without noticing him particularly, she crossed to a corner of the room, and took her whip, which happened to be left there.

"Why in so great a hurry? The nights are as light as day; it matters little when we start. Gertrude, I have something to say to you."

He held out his hand, and drew her upon his knee; at the same time he attracted her attention to a small volume which lay open upon the table.

" Have you read that book ?"

" No, I think not, papa; I do not recollect the title."

" I wish you to read it, then. It contains a singular account of a man who was committed to take his trial for perpetrating a fearful crime. Instead of being sentenced to the gallows, he was banished to the silver mines, to live in them and die there a lingering death. He was deserted, scorned by all his friends save one member of his family. That member followed him to the mines, and preferred working like a beast of burden in a malignant atmosphere with him, to remaining in a home of luxury without his society. Here was an instance of strong and enduring love; was it not, Gertrude?"

"Yes, dear papa; but I should think there are many such instances in the world's history. Love, the bread of life, is unlike anything else; it is limitless as to what it can accomplish."

"Yet, Gertrude, powerful love is sometimes extinguished, when the object on which it is centred degrades itself by committing crimes. Supposing I had committed a capital offence; would you love me as devotedly as you did before, or would there be any decrease in your affection? Would you spurn me, Gertrude?"

"Why ask such a strange question, papa?"

"No matter how strange; give me an answer, Gertrude. I must have an answer."

Gertrude scrutinized her father's face in no small perplexity. "You never spoke in this wild, absolute way before. What possesses you? Why speak of crime? you are not asking me these questions seriously?"

"Yes, Gertrude, seriously. I am disappointed you do not give me an unhesitating reply. You would go with the world, and point at me, supposing I were a murderer, a hypocrite, or a deceiver, as you once dreaded. It would be the same thing; I should be criminal in your eyes, and you would denounce me, and forsake me in my misfortune."

"How bitter, how cruel of you to say so! It was a speech uncalled for, because you know I would not desert you in misfortune; no, never. You would the more need my sympathy. But why allude to crime, small or great? you are not guilty, nor do you stand in need of such proof of my affection"

"How can you tell that, Gertrude? We have been separated for a year. I may have been thrown into temptations, involved in difficulties, and altogether unworthy of your filial love and devotion. I may have become an object of scorn!"

"Impossible, papa! I wish you would neither talk so, nor imagine such things; no, nor look in this strange, unnatural way. You will make me miserable. I cannot define your motive. You look wretchedly ill, too. What can I do to make you happy and well?"

"Ill? do I look ill, do you say? Well, my child, you look like a spectre yourself. I am the cause; I have frightened you. I ought not to have run on in this random way." He rose hastily. "Come, let us start; we with our pale faces! the ride may do us good."

Gertrude held his hand, and, in a coaxing yet timid manner, entreated him to be himself—for her sake he would.

"Forget what has passed—forget it," he repeated, looking anxiously in her face. "I am sorry I have frightened you. My going to Australia seems to have turned me into a savage, and bewildered my senses; or the salt water has been too bracing for me, and has affected my intellect. Is that it, Gertrude?"

"Not Australia, nor the sea, papa? You have become changed only since you went to London."

"Changed, Gertrude! London has not changed me; I am hypochondriacal, and I must try some effective remedy, or the disease will gain ground until I shall not be able to master it. Now, dearest, let us start. You can hear Nanny, from her pawing the ground with impatience. What a fiery, self-willed tartar she is!" They left the library, and were soon mounted.

To enjoy the coolness of the evening, they took their route by the sea-shore. In the course of their ride, Gertrude asked her father if the property he had lately purchased could be seen from where they were.

"Easily; look straight before you—the point of land stretching towards the north and round to the right, enclosing the fields where you see the fence out of repair, adjoining the gate. Can you distinguish the spot I mean?"

"Yes; the cottages, do they belong to you? I wish I had known that last winter," replied Gertrude, rousing herself from her mental depression.

"Why?"

"I should have felt deeper interest in the poor creatures who inhabit them. We must now recollect they have a claim upon us. I have been told they are wretchedly poor, in a state of semi-barbarism. Their parish church is six miles off, and no chapel between this spot and Angharad. It was Lady Elizabeth's ambition to build a church upon that sloping bank: I wish one could be erected to her memory."

"What! a church, Gertrude? A chapel would be far more appreciated. You forget what chapel-goers the Welsh are."

"Yes, but you know the reason: there are so few churches, and a sad dearth of energetic pastors. Were we to build more churches, and have some earnest, disinterested men, who would not neglect their parishes, I feel convinced the chapels would quickly diminish. On this account I am desirous to put my plan into execution. Could we not get up a subscription to erect a simple edifice? It would be conferring a benefit on this little community. The farmers among the hills could also avail themselves of public worship, of which, sad to say, they are now deprived. Anarawd Gwynne, and a few others, I know would be ready to assist. Shall I begin with you, who are always willing to aid any public charity? What will you give me?—give me the land, and endow it. Would that be too great a demand? I am a bold beggar."

"No, Gertrude, not at all: were I to interest myself about the church, I would ask no help. I should prefer building and endowing it at my own expense; or put it into your hands, and let it be exclusively your own bounty, as it is your own proposition."

Doubtful if he were in earnest, Gertrude remarked, that it would come to a great sum; had he thought of that? Besides, no one would expect him to undertake the whole expense.

" What the world expects, or does not expect, is of no moment to me, Gertrude. I act from other motives,—higher motives, I trust. If it will give you real pleasure to carry out your project, and you are sure it will be benefiting the country, I acquiesce without hesitation. I will immediately place you in a position to draw upon my banker for whatever sums are necessary for such a work."

In expressing her gratitude, joy sparkled in Gertrude's eyes. Her father contemplated her in silence; he had not seen so joyous an expression in her face for a long while, but, in his melancholy mood, he made no remark. As they came back from the beach, and passed in front of the cottages, Captain Lewis said he should step in and ascertain from the inhabitants themselves what their feelings were with regard to building the church. It would be as well to hear their opinion.

On approaching the miserable-looking hovels, heaps of cockle-shells lay piled up not a yard distant from the doors. Little ragged urchins and half-starved curs were running about in all directions; and the children's excited voices joining in chorus with the ceaseless barking of the dogs, was deafening. Captain Lewis immediately dismounted, and stooping under a low doorway, he disappeared into one of the cottages. Gertrude, in the mean while, amused herself by watching the children digging pits in the sand. Some were making houses, decorated with broken china and shells, models of their own wretched abodes, probably the only ones they had ever beheld.

Ragged, poverty-stricken, and squalid as they were, it had no effect on their spirits. With their faces beaming with innocent mirth, they danced about in the loose sand, tossing it about with their naked feet in great glee.

"Happy creatures!" thought Gertrude. "Their wants are few. How comparative is all happiness! They feel no oppression at the consciousness of having done wrong, nor persevere in a course they know to be wrong; a slap or an angry look from their mother restores order. Their tears flow, and are dried up, leaving no trace of their sorrow. No care sits upon their hearts. Well may they be happy, far happier than myself! Yet, I was once like them, unfettered and full of glee, with a brighter home and brighter prospects!"

Overjoyed as Gertrude was at her father's unexpected generosity in reference to the church, it did not lighten the oppression at her heart, nor obliterate her unhappy thoughts. Her father's singular conduct previous to their starting, his waywardness, his peculiar expressions so foreign to him, were all too fresh in her mind to let her have a moment's repose. The more she reflected, the worse it appeared to her. She was alarmed at her own conjectures, puzzled at the present and apprehensive about the future.

Since Captain Lewis's return, Anarawd Gwynne had been desirous of coming to Wales for the purpose of obtaining his consent to their union, but had not been able to get leave from his regiment; still he hoped to do so in a few weeks. Gertrude grew impatient to see him. She knew that when he arrived, she would be relieved from the burden of her secret, and her father, as well as they, would know the worst. However ill things might turn out, perhaps it would be better than suspense; still her heart shrank within her, and she was racked by her reflections. Much as she yearned for her lover's presence, she did at times dread his arrival, on account of his interview with her father and the uncertainty of its result. With these forebodings, how could she feel happy? It was hypocrisy to appear so.

Again she glanced at the merry little group, and envied them a peace of mind for which she would have given worlds.

"I am glad I stopped here," said Captain Lewis, as he vaulted into his saddle. "I never came across a more complete picture of wretchedness. I have been continually annoyed with Angharad, from the people rejecting what I would do for them. This Gertrude, shall be my hobby now. No Herbert Gwynne here to interfere with me, I shall have it all my own way. Before I have completed my plan, you will not know the place. It well needs reform."

Gertrude rejoiced to hear there was a prospect of raising the inhabitants from their present deplorable state. As they rode away, she remarked that there were no rosy cheeks nor robust children that they had so often noticed in other villages—they might say, all other villages but this poverty-stricken hamlet.

"Accumulated filth and damp are the cause. They tell me the roofs are in such ill repair, that it is almost impossible in wet weather to keep their beds and themselves dry."

"Poor creatures! It is a marvel how they live in that miserable state without trying to remedy the misery: man hugs it sometimes, I believe. Were I in their places, I should strive by some means to make my home more comfortable, even if I climbed upon the roof and mended it myself."

"That is the spirit they most lack. They want arousing to a sense of their wretched condition. As long as they can fill their mouths with oat-cake and potatoes, they are contented. They are indeed in a half-savage state. We must civilize them. They must be educated. So here is more work for me, though I did not bargain when I bought the property for a community of paupers. We require a long purse in districts such as these, and need never be at a loss how to spend money."

The night was unusually soft and pleasant. The roaring of the sea was heard in the distance. The corn-crakes in the long grass were calling to each other, symptomatic of evening in the delightful season. The equestrians relapsed into silence, as if they were soothed by it; nor were they roused from their reverie till their horses themselves broke into an unbidden canter across the fields. Soon afterwards they followed the road leading directly homewards.

Captain Lewis opening the gate, they passed through, and Gertrude first broke the silence.

" Will the church ever be built, dear papa? Will the pleasure you design ever be conferred upon me? A feeling has come over me that it will never be realized; I cannot help it. I am like a child looking at the weather, upon the fineness of which some promised event depends, alarmed lest a cloud should rise between me and the sun, and disappoint my anticipated joy."

"I hope not. Rather let us look forward to seeing the work before long in a state of progression; the foundations dug, the walls rising, and we on our route there to survey it."

"Delightful! I hope it may be so. With such an object, how doubly pleasant our rides will be!"

"I rejoice to give you pleasure; I have always done so. You have a heart, my little Gertrude, to appreciate what is conferred."

"Why did you finish that sentence with a heavy sigh, papa? It went to my heart. There must be something to cause that depression."

"There would be a greater chance of

happiness in the world, could our hearts be worn upon our faces, Gertrude," he replied, despairingly. " You tax me with being changed; I deny it. What a fool I am! The charge is too just; I am changed. My going to Australia has been a curse to me; nothing has since gone right. Oh! what would I give now if I had never quitted Clogwyn for a week, or even a day! Something does hang over me which I cannot shake off, or explain to you. Man often plants a thorn in his own breast, and heaven knows I have planted a giant thorn in mine."

At that moment they turned a corner in the road, and two gentlemen on horseback came in view. Gertrude immediately recognised one of them as Mr. Gwynne. Her salutation as he passed was acknowledged by one of his courteous bows, his hat raised a foot from his head, but he did not speak.

A few minutes had scarcely elapsed, when they were startled by the sound of a horse galloping up the road in their rear, and a voice called out—

" Why, Lewis, it was so dark; and I, not much of a lynx even in daylight, did not recognize you. How are you, my old friend? We seem to stumble upon each other in all parts of the globe. I have not a moment to spare; so must name my errand, and be off. I have some important business to transact with you. Can I see you to-morrow?—fix your own time."

" Any hour from ten to six."

" Eleven? shall we say eleven?"

" Agreed!" said Lewis, as if the words nad been delivered by machinery rather than the voice.

" I am staying with Herbert Gwynne. I shall only be here a day or two. A bird of passage, as usual!—A bird of passage! Lovely weather!—Good night!"

" That, papa, was the gentleman you met in London," said Gertrude, as the horse's hoofs died in the distance.

"It was, Gertrude: and to me it has proved an evil day—a day of dark omens, as I then felt it was. But I must bear it like a man—our destiny is not in our own hands."

Not another word passed. To Gertrude his silence was painful. She longed to read his features, and express her sympathy; while her mind was distracted by confused and agitated thoughts. This strange gentleman, there could be no doubt, was in some way connected with her father, and was the cause of his troubled spirit. It was from that source he had hinted at difficulties. Was there, then, truth in his words? Had he really done something wrong, requiring a court of justice to decide upon it? In that case, what sorrow might fall upon them! She shuddered at so painful a thought entered her mind. She knew, now, he had real cause for being miserable—that it was not any jealous feeling which she had imagined at times had ruffled his temper. Her heart melted into sympathy with him. He had been in trouble and distress, while she had not striven to soothe and comfort him.

On reaching Clogwyn, Captain Lewis took Gertrude off her horse, previous to the groom's approach. Holding her for a moment in his arms, he pressed his lips to her cheek with a more fervent manner than usual.

"Good night, my dearest Gertrude," said he, dropping his voice. "I shall not see you again this evening."

"Not have a cup of tea after your long ride? Oh, papa, don't leave me alone! If you are in trouble, let it be mine as well as yours." She attempted to retain him.

"No, Gertrude; let me go." He passed on, entered the library, and turned the key.

The sound grated harshly upon Gertrude's ear. She sank into a chair in the hall, and did not move till Yarico came to remind her the tea had been upon the table an hour, and it was time to go to bed.

Gertrude heard the clock strike successively, one, two, three—the library door was still unopened. The sound of her father's step moving about caught her ear once or twice, and all was again still. She could not sleep; and getting up, went to the window, and watched the thread of light on the eastern horizon breaking into day. The air was balmy and calm. A faint rustling among the leaves, and a few sea-birds' screams, were the only sounds which at intervals broke upon the ear.

"The door is opened at last! Dearest papa, I long to go and beg him not to make himself unhappy! If I could only say one word, and look at his dear face for a moment, I am sure I should sleep and feel more comfortable. Perhaps I might cheer him."

As he came by her door, he stopped an

listened. In a few seconds, Gertrude's arms were round his neck.

"Gertrude!"

"I cannot sleep: I have come to repeat good-night, and to beg you will not make yourself miserable about anything. It pains me to see you depressed. Why will you not tell me, my dear father, what your troubles are? You say you wish we wore our hearts upon our faces. That cannot be; but you can give me your confidence."

"Not to-night, my dear. Why did you come out at this hour to look at my haggard features? They ought to dwell out of the light, away from all eyes. I think I do wear my heart upon my face. I cannot conceal the gloom that has come over me. Take away your eyes, Gertrude—go back to bed."

"Say you will not banish me when you are in trouble. We want each other's sympathy; we cannot live happily without it. I cannot be your adviser, but I can offer you my sympathy. That you shall have, and I will be more attentive and forbearing than I have been for some days past. I feel I have not been as kind to you as I ought to have been. I have been ruffled at trifles, and have, I know, often annoyed you. Pray forgive me."

"Do not talk about forgiveness. If things have not gone right this week, it is my own fault; no blame attaches to you. Go to bed, my child; it makes me worse to look at your dear little face. To-night it is more than I can bear!"

He moved onward along the passage to his own room, his frame seeming to totter under its weight.

Gertrude looked after him wistfully, and retired more puzzled than ever about her beloved parent.

CHAPTER XII.

THE stranger had visited Clogwyn, and was gone. All that, to her, long dreary day, Gertrude never saw her father. She waited breakfast for him, but he never made his appearance. She went and listened at his door twenty times. He sent peremptory orders that he would not be disturbed that day.

Bed-time arrived, and her father did not come as usual to wish her good-night. She fretted till nature became exhausted, and with a sorrowful heart retired to her chamber.

Some days passed in painful suspense. Gertrude was sitting alone in the drawing-room at twilight. She was watching her father's restless steps, as he walked upon the terrace backwards and forwards, in the same melancholy mood he had exhibited of late. He was neither smoking, nor sought her company, lovely and inviting as the evening was. Why would he still persevere in keeping her in ignorance of the cause of his distress? How different he was on his first return home! Much agitated, tears gushed into her eyes: she rose, went to the piano, and began playing one of her father's favourite pieces. She could not sing; the power to do so was gone; but the grief which had for so many days been pent up and indulged in silence found utterance in the notes she struck, which penetrated more to the heart than the language of the lips.

When she had played the air over once or twice, and was about to leave the instrument, she observed her father's tall figure standing at her side.

"Play it again, Gertrude," said he.

She immediately complied; and when she

had concluded, the same request was again repeated, and then again. Anxious as she was to please him, she could not go through it the last time. She was overcome: rising hastily, she sank upon the sofa, and vainly endeavoured to restrain her tears.

Captain Lewis took his seat by her side. They sat together for an hour: in that short time all estrangement was gone; Gertrude was in some degree comforted, notwithstanding her father said he must go, and would not have tea.

At breakfast on the following morning, the footman brought in the letters. They came unexpectedly, and Captain Lewis, uttering an exclamation of surprise, turned pale. With a hasty glance, and a nervous shaking of the hand, as he read the address of one of the letters, he put it aside. This did not pass unnoticed by Gertrude. From the moment of its appearance till he left the room, not another syllable escaped his lips. Gertrude looked anxiously after him as he hurriedly crossed the hall with the unopened letter in his hand.

"To-day will seal my fate!" said he, as he entered the library and closed the door. "I shall at least be released from the torture of suspense."

Fortunately Gertrude had by the same post received a letter from Anarawd, and was thus diverted from dwelling upon her father's singular conduct. The letters of her lover never failed to bring her comfort. There was a tone of sincerity about them that always had a salutary effect, while their freshness and originality cheered her even in the present troubled state of her mind.

How many times she wandered round the garden that day with the letter in her hand! How many times she wished she could borrow a magic wand to set all the miserable perplexities straight by which she was so beset! If she could only reason calmly with her father, and he could participate in her future prospects, it would be securing happiness to them all. Anarawd would be a son to him as affectionate as he had been to his mother; for her sake he would, and she herself would never neglect him more than she did now. All this appeared clear to her; but then there was his jealousy of disposition. Were all fathers as jealous? No; because all fathers were not so devoted, few fathers were as devoted as hers. She was therefore ready to admit that it would be a harder struggle for him to part with her. She was an only child, too; he would be desolate without her. She had felt that from the beginning, and the same feeling was now stronger than ever. Still, Anarawd had said much in his letter that was so reasonable, so just, so encouraging: if her father would but listen to him, her fears would vanish.

When dinner was served and the master did not appear, grief came again into her heart. The letter of her lover lost its flattering effect.

"Take the dinner away," said she, turning from the table, "and bring me some tea. I would rather have that."

From the tea-table she went to the terrace, and remained till the sun had set. The shadows grew darker and darker, and the wind came up from the sea and moaned among the trees. All was solitary and dreary, and she hurried back into the house.

The footman had just taken lights into the library. The moment he was gone out of the hall, she went softly to the library door and asked, "May I come in?"

"Yes."

Little did she dream what was impending before she should again cross that threshold.

Her father was sitting in his usual place; letters and papers in great disorder were strewed upon the table. His address to her set her at ease, though before so anxious.

"I am glad you are come; the last hour has been wearisome."

"You did not wish to be disturbed; I was afraid to come."

"I wanted you."

She sat upon his knee; he kissed her, appearing unusually calm.

"You have had better news than you expected, I hope, and are happier, dear papa?"

"News too decided, Gertrude; as to my happiness, that rests in others' hands. Before many days have expired, my joy or my misery will be sealed."

"Papa!"

"You must not be startled! Be prepared, my dear Gertrude, to hear strange facts in connection with ourselves. I have never related to you your true history, and my own only in part. You have been a witness of my distress of mind since I met that gentleman in London. Of the real agony I have endured, you can form no adequate conception. I am glad it is passed, though deeply grieved the time has arrived I am obliged to break to you that which through my life it has been my wish and intention to keep secret."

Gertrude clung to her father, and hid her face upon his shoulder. What secret was going to transpire?

"The gentleman you saw the other day was the only being in the world, besides Yarico and another, who was in possession of my secret: he has betrayed me. He might have had some consideration for my feelings; he might have left the matter in my own hands; but he is a worshipper of the great and wealthy. He would not serve a friend more than a foe, were it to interfere with his own selfish interests. My former hopes are shipwrecked, I fear, without hope for the future. Heaven spare me!"

He paused, moved Gertrude from his shoulder, and looked anxiously in her face.

"You shall hear all presently, and learn how I have deceived you. Yes, Gertrude!

deceived you, and others connected with you. Yet forgive me, my little girl, my joy, my comfort through life, forgive me! Do not be grieved or shocked when I disclose to you that we are in no way connected by blood; I am not your father, and your relations are seeking to separate us. You now have the clue to my grief. What would my life be without the little one I have cherished, and the only being for whom I have lived fifteen long years. How shall I support it?"

"They shall not separate us; you shall be my father still," cried Gertrude, in great agitation.

"Your family is highly connected, and is incensed at my conduct; they won't hear of it, Gertrude. I have done what I ought not strictly to have done, no doubt; yet, could every detail of the case be given retrospectively, excuses would be found for me, and many would be ready to admit that your family are not treating me well It is only what I might expect in this world of insincerity, pride, and ignorance, and the unequal division of society. It is hard for a man to make truth appear to be truth, and justice, justice. One is too often obliged to submit to be insulted and trampled upon by those who arrogate the title of betters—betters in point of blood, not morals, not intellect, not principles, but in a fanciful position arrogant, and boasting of blood with ancestry spotted by plebeian intrigues. I would go to law to-morrow if I could see a chance of gaining my cause; and as to money, I would sacrifice thousands to keep my Gertrude. But there is no such chance. I have too many foreign ties, too few friends at court, and fierce foes in Lord Morlif and Mr. Gwynne, who are prejudicing your friends against me. Independent of these obstacles, the law pampers and favours the nobility—a plebeian is powerless. England calls herself free. She is not free; she is chancery-ridden, law-oppressed. Lawyers make laws and call it the common law. Of statute law I do not speak, but of what the judges fabricate. Thus, my dearest Gertrude, on your relations compelling me to give you up, they will break the cord which has bound us. Never can it be united again. You shall see the correspondence which has passed, and through that you will have a clear insight into the whole affair. You will allow my position is a painful one. But to proceed to events more particularly in connection with ourselves. You have heard me speak of young Fitzhammon and his wife, whom I met in Australia, and with whom I was closely intimate. I have told you repeatedly what friends we were, and how deeply I grieved that he, poor fellow, met with an untimely end, when we went upon that dangerous excursion up the country. You also know how, previous to that melancholy event, he was half distracted and prostrated by his wife's death. With the particulars of those events you are familiar, and must remember how frequently those individuals were the subjects of our conversation. You will now see my motive for endeavouring to make you take an interest in them. Gertrude, they were your real parents. After their decease I became the guardian and protector of their offspring. A short time before your father breathed his last, in the presence of that Mr. Wallet, the gentleman we met the other day, he asked me to take charge of his little girl, bring her to England, and place her in the hands of his eldest brother, then Mr. Fitzhammon, now Lord Strangford. I promised him faithfully I would attend to his wish, and at the time I had no intention of violating that promise. I did break it, and in a worldly sense I have greatly wronged you, my dearest Gertrude, by keeping you out of a sphere higher than my own. I deceived you in leading you to suppose I was your parent, lower and inferior in rank as I am to yourself. In these points

I admit I have been to blame, and merit censure from yourself and family. Yet, Gertrude, let me entreat you to hear my defence before you judge and condemn me."

"This is a fearful blow, indeed!" cried Gertrude, interrupting him, in a voice that penetrated to his soul.

"I have deceived you, Gertrude; I knew this would be a shock. You will never feel the same regard towards me again. Oh, Gertrude, Gertrude, this is what I have dreaded and recoiled from! Yet, much as I deserve your contempt, and do reproach myself, let me not hear it from your lips— spare me, my little Gertrude!"

Gertrude sobbed convulsively, and was unable to articulate a syllable; while he, in a distracted state, continued—

"Hear my defence, hear the simple facts —the quicker they are told the better. When I returned from that ill-fated expedition, I started for Adelaide, where you had been left by your father under Yarico's charge. I brought you with me to Sydney, from which port I sailed for Naples. At that time, you will remember, I was in distress about my unfortunate sister, on account of her ill-fated connection with Lord Morlif. It was impossible to describe my bitter detestation of the aristocracy. The odious specimens of it I met at Paris were ever present to my memory: hence, I looked upon all to be equally immoral, unprincipled, and reckless. I was, perhaps, more attached to your father on account of his being ill-treated by the same unhealthy class. He had given his family mortal offence by marrying a clergyman's daughter. To escape their persecution, and ensure the means of obtaining a fortune as a farmer, he came out to Australia to fight his way, and be independent of his titled connections. He was altogether an exception to the poor creatures of his class I met in Naples and Paris. I never became acquainted with a more generous, noble-hearted fellow. We were like brothers. My friendship for him kept me longer in Australia than I should otherwise have been. For his sake, I first loved his child, and then for her own. I need hardly tell you I was a young man at that time—a wild, hardy fellow, tossed about the world like a football—fond of my ship, and fond of adventure. You can imagine that when I had a fairy-like child, a little engaging thing, placed especially under my guardianship, it was a singular and odd position in which to find myself. I knew nothing of children's habits and ways, or how they win upon the heart. During the voyage you became my study and amusement. Yarico will tell you what a violent fancy you took to me from the first moment you saw me, and the struggles there were to get you to leave me and go to her. You were ill for some days during the voyage, and we thought you would have died. Had I been your parent, I could not have felt more anxious about you. Somehow, Gertrude, you wound yourself round my heart in an unaccountable manner—your laughing blue eyes were my delight. I used to sit for hours watching your movements with a fascination not to be described. It so happened, when I was one evening walking upon the deck, you fell asleep in my arms. I recollect how struck I was with your innocent face, half buried in your soft flaxen hair. Then it was a sudden resolution seized me, that I would not take you to England to be contaminated and blighted by the bad atmosphere which surrounds high life, but that I would adopt you, and that my fortune, which was an increasing one, should be bestowed upon you. I would never marry, but devote myself to you, and endeavour to make your life a happier existence than that of a dependent upon brainless, high-born relations, which, with your sensitive nature, you would feel acutely. You should never know what you gained, or what you lost. I argued thus; and dwelt, perhaps, too much upon my plans, without considering, as I ought to have done, the unfair advantage I was taking of the trust committed to me, as well as the infringement of the promises given to your father on his deathbed. I perceive now, more than I did then, it was not an upright, any more than a politic act. Yet, dearest Gertrude, fate had willed it so. I did commit the offence; and never from that time till I saw Mr. Wallet (who, I thought, in all likelihood would have lived and died in Australia,) did I feel the smallest compunction or regret for the deed. My love and increasing solicitude for my stolen child, steeled my conscience against all scruples. Stolen waters were sweet to me. Your defencelessness, your dependence upon me for happiness, were secret gratifications, and a continued pleasure. All your wants were met, and I was most desirous your education should not be neglected, nor your spirits damped. But I will say no more—the rest is within your knowledge."

His voice was tremulous; and with some effort, he resumed—

"Those letters, Gertrude, you had better see them, shocked as you will be to read what motives they attribute to my actions. God knows, and you know, how grossly they wrong me. I care little for their insults or their reproaches. Yours, my little Gertrude, only yours, I dread. I shrink from apprehension that you have not one word of forgiveness for me. Do reproach and indignation overwhelm all affection?"

"No, no, you misunderstand me," cried Gertrude in tones of deep distress. "I neither condemn nor reproach you, nor can anything change my feelings towards you. If you have wronged me, it has long been obliterated by your love, kindness, and care. I harbour no regrets; none but this, to my sorrow, that you are not my father."

" You forgive me, then?"

" Freely, dearest papa."

He held her to his heart for some minutes, blessed and thanked her.

Again and again Gertrude solicited her father not to permit her relations to take her from him; that it would break her heart to leave him, and live among strangers.

" I have no natural tie to bind you; the law cannot help me. I fear, my dearest Gertrude, it must be so. This is the source of my sorrow; this has been gnawing at my heart ever since I met that man's face. I had a presentiment he would betray me, for I knew his family were intimate with the Gwynnes in London."

" Let me read those letters," said Gertrude, rising and looking as pale as ashes.

They were placed in her hand in succession of dates. With great endeavour to compose herself, she commenced their perusal—not an easy task—with new feelings struggling within her, and still trembling under a shock from which it would take a long time to recover.

When she finished reading the letters, she made no comment upon them. She did not open her lips again, but her distress was painful. Captain Lewis was greatly moved. With almost the tenderness of a mother to a sick child, he entreated her to go to bed. He conducted her to her room, kissed her affectionately, and used all his endeavours to comfort her, he himself needing comfort more than she did.

When he returned to the library, the stillness of the room was painful to him. His mind was too unsettled to write a letter which he wished to despatch. His hands were tremulous, and his brain in confusion. He went down to the beach and leaped into his boat, for he was ever at home upon the sea. It would not soothe him, but it would be more supportable there than were he in bed.

Soon he was bounding over the waves in the direction of his yacht. A few minutes more, and he was pacing his deck, solitary and undisturbed.

Clogwyn rose upon the summit above the cliff, an elephantine, dark, shapeless mass. There was not a gleam of light from any of the windows in the house, yet it seemed the main object of his attraction. He was glad no light came from Gertrude's casement, and that her head was upon the pillow. To see her prostrated with grief had been a bitter pain to him, for her tears lacerated his heart. They had always, from her early childhood, had an effect upon him, but now they were unnerving and insupportable. That he should be the cause of her sorrow, distressed him deeply; and that he had committed such a mistake in his life's history, was but secondary to that reflection.

He stood with his eyes directed upon his home. The brightest and happiest hours of his life had been spent there. Gertrude had been a part of himself, the one tie in life. Could he hold the moment fast, and keep the hour back when he must lose her, forsake his home, and abandon himself to the wide world again? Was there no hope, no means to avert the coming evil? She had forgiven him his deception of her. She had assured him the revelation of her history should work no change in her affection. But would she, for his sake, give up all for him— be still his? Delusive aspirations! gossamer threads! to be blown away at a breath! They must part, let the conflicting feelings be what they might!

Had she a partiality for Anarawd Gwynne? the thought had sometimes troubled him. He had noticed the colour come into her cheeks when he had mentioned the name. But, then, had not Gertrude ever been a blushing little thing, young, and impulsive too? Why put such a construction on her actions? Had anything existed between them, she would have confessed it to him, confiding in him as she had ever done. Besides, a Gwynne—a Gwynne of Bleddyn, would not contemplate a union with one whom the world supposed his daughter. Their pride was in their blood. They would sacrifice peace for that idle notion. They would hazard a life of martyrdom for blood and social position. He knew Gwynne's views; and though in reality he was himself a scion of as good a stock as his, Gwynne would not acknowledge it, nor allow his son to do so either. They boasted it was never known that a Gwynne contracted a marriage with an inferior in standing. He was safe there. His fears arose from jealousy; and yet he had no cause to complain of want of affection in Gertrude. He believed it was as deep-seated as ever it had been, while her daughterly devotion to him had never been exceeded. Had not misfortune come upon them, he could see nothing to intercept their peace to the end of life. They might have lived, as they had done before, in uninterrupted happiness.

He placed his hand on his forehead. Thoughts crowded afresh upon his brain. His perturbation increased.

"I must lose her! I must lose her!" he repeated in tones of keen suffering. "My thoughts fret and wear me; they chop about like a vessel driven by every changing gust to another point of the compass. It is hard to weather such storms—to keep the helm under command. I must come back to my yacht, that will screen me from the world's gaze, and my little Gertrude will not witness my sufferings. On board I shall have much to remind me of her. Memory is a friend, as well as a foe; it will recall her laughing eyes to cheer my loneliness. Fancy will sometimes bring again to my ear that voice, the sweetest I ever heard. These must be my consolation. These will help me to fill up the dreary waste, the wide void in my soul, which I dread more than a hundred storms in the Bay of Biscay."

The dawn lagged; the enlightening sky began to be faintly reflected in the ocean. Pilot-boats issued from the creek, a little below Angharad. Roused from his reflections, Captain Lewis once more leaped into his boat, and setting up his sprit-sail, for there was a gentle breeze, he stood out to sea. For an hour or two he continued to work his way against wind and tide. Suddenly he thought to run back to the shore, and looked up, as if expecting to see cliffs where there were none. With a bewildered aspect he turned away; he was not under Clogwyn. What possessed him to suppose he had reached home, when he had been all that while sailing in a contrary direction? He believed his senses were forsaking him; how else could he account for his mis-reckoning? God was surely punishing him for idolatry, in fixing his affections on Gertrude as he had done. He had no religion in his heart;

that which he had mistaken for religion was not the reality. He had followed erroneous principles. He had been grasping pleasure with one hand, and working his own ruin with the other. All the good he had endeavoured to do in this world produced only diseased, unwholesome fruit—fruit withering and perishing before it had reached maturity. Punishment came upon men in dark and strange shapes. Punishment had come to mock him; to remind him of his presumption; to trample him down to his level; to make him see what he would not see, that he was no demi-god of the earth, but a miserable, hopeless, humiliated creature!

The boat was put about, and taking his seat in the stern sheets, he floated it down with the tide to Clogwyn.

A letter arrived the same morning from Lord Strangford, stating he should send two of his servants on a fixed day to meet and conduct his niece to London. Other preliminary matters were mentioned, and a request added that there might be no interference with the arrangements.

Gertrude, in great grief, gave orders for her things to be packed. She walked about half unconscious of her position, and could scarcely imagine what was about to be realised. She could not look at her guardian without a flood of tears, and yet was more miserable when separated from him. She had a great aversion to going among her relations, and was the more prejudiced against them on account of their having treated Captain Lewis so ill.

In a week she became more reconciled, or rather it should be said, collected. She hinted to Captain Lewis that they were only parting for a time, she should soon be her own mistress by the law of the land. Her relations, too, should know his worth, and acknowledge how much they had wronged him. He must very often come to see her, and those moments would still be precious to her. She would never do anything without his consent, and seek his counsel in preference to all others. He would, in her estimation, be ever her father.

Many similar things to these he listened to, but they failed to convey to him a ray of consolation.

The days they were thus passing together for the last time, were a period of painful trial to both, because each moment something occurred to remind them of their approaching separation. Constant packing was going on. Captain Lewis had given Gertrude, from time to time, many valuable presents, all of which he wished her to take away. It was no slight undertaking to get all ready. The preparations, too, excited him to frenzy. He could not attend to his own affairs. He had settled to leave Clogwyn as soon as Gertrude had taken her departure.

Upon one occasion, before she departed, he went into what had been once her school-room. Yarico had been rummaging out the closets, and her playthings and story-books lay promiscuously upon the floor. He picked up one of the books, recognising it as a gift to Gertrude when a child. It had been a great favourite of hers —so great, she would never go to bed without her treasure under her pillow. Memory brought back that, and many similar incidents, to torture him. In the general confusion of packing, the book was not thought of, it had long ceased to be regarded; with youth more advanced, years brought new toys, friendships, joys, and hopes. He fancied, in like manner, that he too would soon be forgotten and thrown aside in that whirlpool of gaiety and dissipation into which she was about to be immersed. He took the book and put it into his bosom. " Oh, the vanity of man ! One motive for adopting my little Gertrude, was to keep her unsullied from the alluring vanities of high life. What is the termination of all, of my earnest desires and parental care? A blow from that awful and mysterious Hand, which we all feel, but cannot see, has shattered my expectations, alas! never more to be fulfilled; their ruin sending me adrift upon the world, like a hulk upon the stormy sea, and my little Gertrude thrown into the vortex from which I had snatched to preserve her. That God's ways are not man's ways, is here forcibly illustrated. God is just; men are not rewarded according to their vices and virtues. Some, vile enough, dance over the world upon a golden thread; others, the more virtuous of their kind, have to drag out their existence in fetters, to strive and labour, while fortune frowns upon them to their last hour. Bread is not given to the wise, nor riches to men of understanding, nor favour to men of skill! such is man's mysterious destiny in this lower world. For myself, I have been favoured by Fortune; yet better would it have been never to have received her smiles, than to pay this heavy penalty, banished, as I shall be, for ever from my life's joy—left alone, a solitary being, bereft of all I valued in existence."

With the shutters partly open, in the most retired and desolate-looking of any room in the house, he lingered before those toys and playthings of Gertrude's childish years, those touching reminiscences of departed moments whose value when present was so little esteemed. The thoughts of the coming separation became almost overwhelming. His senses seemed to reel, and he leaned forward to support himself against the chimney-piece.

In this distressing state Gertrude found him. She entered the room, but he did not hear her footstep, so much was he absorbed in his sorrow, nor was he aware of her presence until she was close to his side.

" What has brought you here? Keep

away, my child; keep away from me, in mercy! Gertrude, I have lost control over myself; I can support it no longer."

She threw her arms around his neck and wept. At another time her caresses would have been returned, they were now tortures.

" Why will you persist?" said he, half angrily, pushing her from him. "It is mockery to offer me consolation, your voice and presence aggravate my sorrow. Are you not going to leave me to my fate? Are we not parting to meet no more?"

" No more! The saddest words of all, my dearest father. You could not be so cruel, after parting, not to come and see me. If my relations forbid your visiting me, I have told you before, I will not live with them. They shall permit you to see me, and you will often come."

" No, Gertrude, I could not see you in that new sphere, amid such conventional society, that atmosphere of studious coldness, hollow drawing-room smiles, and laborious politeness. To meet my little girl in that uncongenial air would give me little pleasure. You could not be what you once were to me. My heart shrinks from it. I should see you unlearning there, too, all the lessons I have taught you of truth and sincerity."

There was silence on both sides for a few moments, and he continued—

"Why will you leave me, Gertrude—why permit any one to intermeddle with our happiness? you declared you would never forsake me in misfortune, that I should then require your sympathy the more, and you would give it me. Could a greater calamity befall me than the present? yet, my child, you are leaving me to my fate!"

"I would not leave you were it in my power to avoid it. You know how miserable I am at parting from you—how I dread going among my relations; rich as they are, and high-born, they are nothing to me; rank is nothing. You are more to me, dearest papa, than they can ever be. You know I feel this; it is true."

"Why, then, forsake me? The power is yours; make use of that power, and let not my future life be one of sorrow. Have you no feeling, no pity, no love in return for my paternal regard? Think, Gertrude, what I have been to you through life, a devoted parent, living solely for you. What would that life be without you?"

"I do not understand you. What would you have me do? I am not yet of age."

He walked frantically about the room for some minutes, then approached Gertrude, and placed her upon the sofa by his side.

"Gertrude, you shall understand me. I am goaded to despair. I find it impossible to part from you. Listen to me! Will you, for my sake give up your high-born relations, and bear the world's censure, the law's power? You have placed confidence in me from infancy; still retain that confidence. I swear solemnly, Heaven is my witness, I will never betray that confidence. You shall be still my child."

His voice grew hoarse—" Gertrude, my dear, consent to fly with me; and we will leave this country, and go beyond the reach of your patrician relatives: they shall never know where we are. Trust me, the world's frowns shall not cast a shadow across your path. I will be to you what I have hitherto been, your protector, guardian, and parent. There shall be no dereliction, on my part in performing my duty; or rather, I shall be more anxious about my treasure. With you, I can make my home anywhere; there will, with you, be no regret at leaving Clogwyn. Without you, Gertrude, there will be no home in the wide world for me. I beseech you, then, to listen to my entreaty, and emancipate me from a miserable solitary existence."

Gertrude's head sank upon his bosom, with burning tears streaming from her eyes. He clasped her to him. " Speak, my best, my dearest of all children; moments are hours of torture to me."

He put his ear near to catch the words as she struggled to articulate. Her lips parted and closed—she could only murmur—

" Anarawd Gwynne."

"What of him? Oh God, Gertrude! tell me what you mean?"

A dead silence succeeded, which was broken by Gertrude's hasty confession.

" I have promised to marry him. I could not fly from him. I could not give him up, and go with you to foreign lands. Blame me if I merit your censure, yet pity me, your wretched child. My heart is torn with anguish. I love you with the same devotion, and shall ever love you, as deeply as a child can love a parent. Do not forsake me, I implore you not to forsake me. I cannot break my pledge and be faithless. Hear me, dearest father, hear me. Do not cast me from you!"

Gertrude never forgot the effect her confession made upon Ricardo Lewis. To convey an idea of what she had to support in witnessing his distress is not possible, for it defies description.

With a bitter cry she sank upon her knees before him, and supplicated his forgiveness. She spoke of her home being still his home, that they should ever be together; would he only consent, they neither of them would be wanting in filial affection to him. It would be their main object to make him happy. He never should see any diminution of her affection, never, never!

Captain Lewis waved his hand impatiently, motioning her to silence. For some moments he could not find utterance. When at length he spoke, his bearing was changed, and his voice came upon her ear unlike his own—sad, yet marked with severity—

" Torture me no further, Gertrude; you might have spared me much, spare me now. Our separation must be irrevocable—it will be for ever! My love for you, my child, demands more than you can now give me. I could not share your affection; I must have all or none. We must then part to meet no more!"

Again and again Gertrude beseeched him upon her knees not to desert her, and render her life as wretched as his own.

A storm had come up from the sea; the wind blew with the fury of a hurricane against the house, the windows and shutters were shaking to and fro—all was in commotion. Heavy claps of thunder, accompanied by lurid darkness, seemed to drive evening into night. Their figures were scarcely visible to each other, except at those times when the lightning, flashing in their faces, played upon the toys on the floor and illuminated the walls. It was a fearful night, such as is seldom experienced.

In the midst of this tempestuous uproar, Lewis snatched Gertrude from the floor, and held her once more in his arms, as if to shield her from the vivid lightning. At length all was silent; the wind and the thunder died away in the distance. It was during one of these pauses, fearful intervals of the storm, that sadly upon Gertrude's ear came the following exclamation:

"I could curse the man who robbed me of my treasure, my dear, dear, child, the child after my own heart! but that she loves him. There is a stronger passion than filial love — stronger than death, said the wise man. It may be so, and she may forsake me, give me up for ever! For her sake, but only for her sake, I withhold my curse, my bitterest curse, from him who deprives me of her." He held up his hands, and repeated in wild accents, which vibrated through the room—

" God of mercy, give me strength to support this crushing trial! Gertrude, Gertrude, think of my forlorn heart!" He rested his head upon the sofa, and groaned deeply.

His exclamation and accompanying sorrow sank into Gertrude's inmost soul, and became indelibly fixed upon her memory; even at the moment it imparted such a shock to her sensibility, that she became lost to all but the words—" Think of my forlorn heart!"

In after years, when time had cicatrized the grief of the past, she seldom entered that room without leaving a tear, as a tribute to the memory of that heart-rending moment.

Surveying Ricardo Lewis as he stood, with a drawn and frigid expression of features, his frame shrunk, and his hand trembling as he lifts Gertrude, with as little colour in her face as his own, into the carriage, and responds to her last farewell, he can scarcely be recognised as the same light-hearted man who came to Wales in the heyday of his youth, sitting upon the oak-settle at the " Llewelyn ap Griffydd," puzzling Hugh Lloyd with his rhetorical language, or teasing Lloyd's wife about the great folks at Bleddyn: neither could he be recalled for the same person who appeared a few years subsequently to take possession of Clogwyn, accompanied by his little girl, softened in manners, and if not so exuberant in spirits, having a more contented and happy expression. In neither of the two could be traced a resemblance to the sad spectacle of which the parting hour had been the occasion.

During the years he lived in Wales, he had done more good to the small town of Angharad than had ever been done before, notwithstanding Mr. Gwynne's opposition. He had infused new ideas there, established new rules, and had been the means of promoting the education of the youth, as well as a friend to the poor and needy. No one would be more missed or more regretted than the " noble gentleman," as they denominated Captain Lewis of Clogwyn.

At the time of his departure, it was not known in the neighbourhood that he had no intention of returning to Wales, nor that he carried away with him a shattered heart.

The sails of his yacht unfurled, and as it carried him gallantly to sea, he turned to view his home fading in the distance. Not a sigh nor a frown escaped him, not a tear was upon his face; his countenance was as inanimate as a marble bust. The only words which rose upon his memory, but found no utterance, were those which burst from the lips of the great Italian poet when he started on his wanderings—

"*Com' è duro calle!*"

The spider so poetically described by the ancients draws its venom from the rose. Thus it is too often, that from the sweetest sources comes the blight of human affection.

END OF VOL. II.

www.ingramcontent.com/pod-product-compliance
Lightning Source LLC
Chambersburg PA
CBHW030740230426
43667CB00007B/792